151 Moral STORIES

151 Moral Stories

Publisher:

MANOJ PUBLICATIONS

761, Main Road, Burari, Delhi-110084

Ph.   : 27611116, 27611349

Fax   : 27611546, Mob. : 9868112194

email : info@manojpublications.com

For online shopping visit our website : **www.manojpublications.com**

Showroom :

1583-84, Dariba Kalan, Chandni Chowk, Delhi-110006

Ph. : 23262174, 23268216

Mobile : 9818753569

ISBN : 978-81-310-1747-0

CONTENTS

1. *The Dreamer Milkmaid*

Taking a large container of milk on her head a milkmaid was on her way for selling it. As her steps were moving towards the market, her inclination towards wealth was being enhanced. A surge of excitement of money by selling the milk was noticeable. She began to dream how she would dream use that money. She was murmuring the words and moving her hands. Her dream took her in a different world and she said to herself, "The money, after selling the milk, would be used for purchasing a hundred chicks and when chicks would be fully grown, I would sell them at a good price for buying two goats. When the goats would be fully grown, I could sell them at an even better price!" Still dreaming, she said to herself, "Soon, I would be able to buy two more cows and I would have a lot of money with a luxurious life." With these happy thoughts, she began to skip and jump. Suddenly, she tripped and fell. The jug broke and all the milk spilt onto the ground. "No more dream," she cried foolishly.

Moral : Do not count your chickens before they are hatched.

2. The Parched Crow

In the scorching hot day, a crow flew for a long time hither and thither looking for water. He felt too exhausted, almost gave up hope when he couldn't find any water. Suddenly, he saw a pitcher in a field. The pitcher had meagre water. He found impossible to touch the level of water; he tried again and again but couldn't. But his witty mind got an idea. Looking around, he saw some pebbles. He suddenly started picking up the pebbles one by one, dropping each into the pitcher. As the level of the water was moving up, his surge of enthusiasm was also increasing as well. Now the level of water was up enough to touch with

his beak. The crow glugged down the water and his thirst was quenched soon. His satiety, he got by his wit and idea made him really proud of himself.

Moral : One can reach a final destination if one tries hard.

3. The Clever Lamb and the Strong Wolf

Once a lamb was taking pleasure of sweet grass at the edge of the field with a flock of sheep. She was enjoying herself so much that she went farther and farther and didn't notice a wolf coming nearer to her. When she was pounced upon by the wolf, the lamb begged him to wait a while and stated when her stomach was full of grass she would be more tastier. Then he could devour her. Finding this a good idea he sat down and waited. The lamb asked the wolf to permit her to dance, so the grass would be digested faster in her stomach. Again, the wolf agreed. The dancing lamb got a new idea to make him ring the bell as hard as he could, so she could dance even faster. The wolf rang a bell as hard as he could. The shepherd heard the bell ringing and quickly sent his dogs to find the missing lamb. The barking dogs frightened the wolf away and saved the lamb's life.

Moral : A little creature can sometime be dominating.

4. The Devious Wolf in a Sheep's Skin

Once a wolf found a great difficulty to have the vigilance of the shepherd and his dogs. But one day luckily, it found the skin of a sheep that had been flayed and thrown aside, so the wolf with an agile mind decided to put it on over its own pelt. It strolled down among the sheep. The lambs that belonged to the sheep, whose skin the wolf was wearing, began to follow the wolf in the sheep's clothing. The lambs which followed the wolf were taken little apart from the flock. Since the wolf found a good opportunity, it soon made a meal of them. For some time he succeeded in deceiving the sheep, and enjoying hearty meals.

Moral : Sometimes a deceptive but witty brain is useful.

5. A Pit Brimmed with Water

Long ago, a pond was dug by a very affluent king and it was announced that one person from each household would have to bring a glass of milk during the night and pour it into the pond. So, the pond should be full of milk by the morning. After receiving the order, everybody went home. One of the denizens of the kingdom made up his mind to take milk but after pondering for a while he thought, "Since everyone will bring milk, I could pour water in place of milk because it would be hard to see in the twilight." He quickly poured the water and came back. In the morning the king was astonished to see the pond filled with water only. It so happened that everyone thought like the denizen, "I will not pour the milk; someone else will do."

Moral : Don't neglect your duty.

6. The Beautiful Rose and the Thorny Cactus

Once in a beautiful spring rose a pine tree in a forest looked at a red blossomed rose and said, "What a beautiful flower; I wish I were you. The rose said, "It seems that I am the most beautiful plant." Then a sunflower raising its head said there were many plants including the rose which were beautiful. The conceited rose, said looking at a thorny cactus, "What an ugly plant!." Then the rose went ballistic when the pine tree compared the thorns of the rose plant with those of the cactus. The rose raged at the cactus to be his neighbour and infuriatingly tried to move his roots away from the cactus but couldn't. Spring passed and life became difficult when in sweltering hot days plants and animals needed water and there was no rainfall. Once the wilted rose saw sparrows stick their beaks into the cactus and then fly away, refreshed. The rose got puzzled. The tree explained, "The birds got water from the cactus that hurts, but the cactus does not like to see any birds suffer." The rose blushed with shame.

Moral : Never judge anyone by his appearance.

7. Fear of the Lion and the Elephant

Once upon a time , a discussion was going on between a lion, the king of the forest, and his friend, elephant, who was the inhabitant of the same forest. They were talking about their great deeds. Then suddenly, the lion disclosed his fear of the crowing of cocks. The elephant started ridiculing him. Just then, a small mosquito started circling around the elephant's ears making him restless and anxious. The elephant was really scared of its humming that made him perplexed. Now it was the turn of the lion to be amused at the elephant's action.

Moral- Sometime our fear is baseless.

8

8. *Change your View, not World*

Once a king named Chandravahan ruled over an affluent country. One day, he went to hunt animals in some remote area. When he returned back from the trip, he felt too exhausted to move anymore. His felt were sore after a long trip on the rough and gravelled road of distant areas. It was his first trip on road which pained him a lot, so he gave the order to cover the road of his entire country with leather. Definitely, this was a very expensive task to cover the road with leather in which the cow's skin was needed. Then one of his wise servants dared to tell the king, "Why do you have to spend that unnecessary amount of money? Why don't you just cut a little piece of leather to cover your feet?" The king was astounded on this suggestion but later he agreed and decided to make slipper of leather.

Moral : To make this world a happy place to live in, you had better change yourself, your heart, and not the world.

9. *The Perceptive Child*

A fragile and doddering man lived with his son, daughter-in-law, and four-year old grandson. The old man's hands trembled, his eyesight was blurred, and his step faltered. The family ate together at the table. But the elderly grandfather's shaky hands and failing sight made eating difficult. Since the grandfather had broken a dish or two, his food was served in a wooden bowl. His grandson was perceptively observing all this in silence. One evening before supper, the father noticed his son playing with wood scraps on the floor. He asked the child sweetly, "What are you making?" The boy said that he was making a little bowl for the dad and the mom to eat their food in when he would grow up. The words struck the parents terribly. They understood their fault and decided to lead the old man back to the family table.

Moral : Children perceptively observe their surroundings.

10. *A Stranger in Garden*

Once, after diligently hard work, a gardener happily went with his son to his garden to bring the fruits which he had been caring for a long time. As he reached there, he was astounded to see a stranger picking the fruits without informing anybody. He went berserk and shouted, "Hey you! What are you doing on my tree? Aren't you ashamed of stealing fruits?" The stranger replied, "Everything is of God and I am God's servant." This answer baffled him and again he shouted at the stranger. But the stranger continued picking fruits. After pondering, the gardener asked his son to bring a rope and a stick, and began to beat the stranger. "Stop! Stop! What are you doing? Don't you fear God," the stranger cried horribly. "Like you I am also God's servant and this world belongs to God," the gardener prudently added, "So you should not interfere in God's work." Then the stranger realized his mistake and apologized for his deed of stealing fruits.

Moral : Believe in your hard work only.

11. *The Witty Mother Duck and the Greedy Fox*

Once a mother duck with her ducklings was proceeding towards a lake. The ducklings happily followed their mother quacking along the way. Suddenly, she saw a fox in the distance. She got frightened and shouted to move hurriedly to the lake to her ducklings as there's a fox. The ducklings hurried towards the lake. The mother duck pondered what to do. She began to walk back and forth dragging one wing on the ground. When the fox saw her, he became happy. He thought, 'She seemed to be hurt, so I can catch and eat her.' Then he ran towards her. The mother duck ran, leading the fox away from the lake. Now the ducklings were safe; they had reached the lake. She stopped and took a deep breath of relief. As soon as the fox was coming closer to her, she quickly spread her wings and flew away. Finally, she landed in the middle of the lake and joined the ducklings. The fox kept staring at them astonishingly.

Moral : All mothers sacrifice for their children first.

12. The Fox and the Grapes

It was such a scorching day that every animal could hardly get relief. One day, a fox wandered across the jungle in order to get food. Soon he came to a vineyard which was laden with juicy grapes. The fox observed around him to confirm whether he was safe from the hunters or not. He was absolutely ravenous, so he decided to steal some grapes before anyone came along. He jumped again and again as high as he could, but couldn't reach the grapes. The grapes were too high for him. He was not ready to give up. He backed off, took some running steps and leapt into the air towards the grapes. Again, he failed to reach them. It was getting dark, and he was getting angry. His legs hurt with all that running and jumping. At last, he stopped trying and walked away saying he didn't want those grapes. They would be too sour to eat.

Moral : We pretend something to be ugly, if we do not get it.

13. The Assertive Tortoise and the Conceited Hare

Once, a tortoise met a hare who scornfully remarked, "How slowly you move!" This remark seemed to agitate him to take an audacious decision. The tortoise said, "Let's have a race and see who is the faster." The hare contemptuously laughed and said he would reach the other side of the hill first. Off he ran, leaving the tortoise far behind.

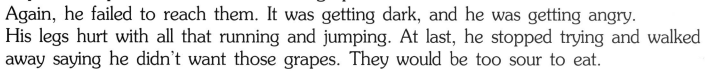

After a while, the hare stopped to wait for the tortoise to come long. He waited and waited till he felt sleepy and decided to take a nap. He dozed under a shady tree and closed his eyes envisaging, 'Even if he would catch me, I can easily win the race.' The tortoise continued the race slowly but steadily and passed the sleeping hare. By the time the hare woke up and ran as fast as he could, the tortoise had become the winner.

Moral : Confidence is good but over-confidence may defeat you.

14. *Debt that cannot be Paid off*

Once a boy hurriedly came up to his mother in the kitchen, and handed her a piece of paper that he had been writing on. Mother became astounded to see and to read that, in which money had been asked, for cutting the grass: $5.00, for cleaning up the room: $1.00, for going to the store: $.50, for taking care of the baby while she had gone to market: $.25, taking out the garbage: $1.00, for getting a good report card: $5.00, for cleaning up and raking the yard: $2.00. Total owed: $14.75. On the back of the paper she wrote–no charge for carrying nine months in stomach, no charge for treatment and praying all night for you during illness, no charge for wiping your nose, no charge for fulfilling your requirements. Total cost: nil. This writing choked the boy and he overwhelmingly said, "Mom, I do love you." And then he took the pen and in great big letters he wrote, "Paid in full."

Moral : Mother's love can't be repaid in money.

15. *A Rock on a Road*

Once upon a time, a king had placed a boulder on a roadway. Then he hid himself and watched to see if anyone would remove the huge rock. Some of the king's wealthiest merchants and courtiers came by and simply walked around it. Many loudly blamed the king for not keeping the roads clear, but none did anything about getting the big stone out of the way. Then a peasant came along carrying a load of vegetables. Approaching the boulder, the peasant laid down his burden and tried to move the stone to the side

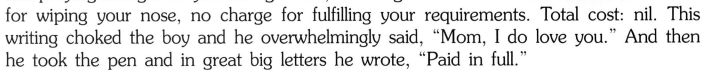

of the road. After much pushing and straining, he finally succeeded. As the peasant picked up his load of vegetables, he noticed a purse lying in the road where the boulder had been. The purse contained many gold coins and a note from the king indicating that the gold was for the person who removed the boulder from the roadway. The peasant learnt what many others never understood.

Moral : Work done selflessly always yields rich dividends.

16. The Son's Crushed Fingers

A man who bought a new car, came to his house to show it to his wife, who was working in the kitchen. But when they came out, they found their son ridiculously hammering a dent in the car. It really infuriated the father who mercilessly hammered the son's hand into pulp as punishment. As he got back his wit, he took his son to a nearby hospital, where in order to save his hand the doctors finally had to amputate the fingers from the boy's both hands.

When the boy woke up from the surgery and saw his bandaged stubs, he innocently said, "Daddy, I'm sorry." Then he asked, "But when are my fingers going to grow back?" The incident tormented the father and he committed suicide. His one evil step not only spoilt his child's hand, but also snatched a father's hand from the child.

Moral : Any action we take in rage may haunt us, so pause and ponder for a while to reach any decision.

17. Deafness becomes a Boon

Once a group of frogs was living contentedly in the woods. Suddenly, some frogs gathered around the pit finding two of them had fallen into a deep pit. When they saw how deep the pit was, they dejectedly told the two frogs in the pit that they should prepare themselves for their fate, because they were as good as dead. Reluctantly, the two frogs began to jump with all their might. Some of the frogs shouted into the pit that it was hopeless, and that the two frogs wouldn't have been in that situation if they had been more careful, more obedient. Listening to them one of the two frogs into the pit lost hope and quietly resolved himself to his fate. He lay down at the bottom of the pit, and died as the others looked on in helpless grief. But another frog kept struggling. Finally,- he leapt so high that he sprang out of the pit. The amazed frogs asked him, "Why he keep jumping as they told him it was impossible?" Reading their lips, the astonished frog told them that he was deaf.

Moral : Sometimes weakness becomes strength.

18. Depth of Understanding

One day, a father of a very affluent family decided to take his son on a trip to show how the poor people lived so he could be thankful for his wealth. They spent a couple of days with poor families. On their return from their trip, the father asked his son, "How was the trip?" "It was great, Dad." "Did you see how poor people can be?" the father asked. "Oh yeah," said the son. "So what did you learn from the trip?" asked the father. The boy said, "We have one dog but they had four; we have a pool that reaches the middle of our garden and they have a creek that has no end; we have imported lanterns in our garden and they have the stars at night; we have a small piece of land, they have fields beyond our sight; we buy our food but they grow theirs; we have walls but they have friends to protect."

The boy thanked his father for showing how poor they were.

Moral : Sometimes children can be source of knowledge.

19. The Farmer and the Stork

Finding a few uninvited cranes destroying his newly sown crops, a farmer set a net in his field in order to catch those destructive birds.

Next day, when the farmer strode across the field to examine the net he found that the net was full of cranes and a stork. Suddenly, the farmer heard a moaning voice of a stork, who was imploring to release him. The stork innocently cried, "I am a poor stork and I have not eaten your crops. I serve my parents with dutiful work." The stork pleaded for life but the farmer cut him short. "All this may be true enough, but you have been caught with those destructive birds so you must suffer the company in which you are found," asserted the farmer.

Moral : Company matters a lot for judgment.

20. *God on Earth*

Once a man started arguing about the existence of God on earth with a barber when he had gone to have his beard and hair cut in a barber shop. The barber said, "Look man, I don't believe that God exists as you say so. If God existed, would there be so many sick people? Would there be abandoned children? If God existed, there would be neither suffering nor pain." The barber finished his job and the client went out of the shop.

Just after he had left the barber shop, he saw a man in the street with long hair and a beard. Then the client again entered the shop with the long-bearded man and said to the barber, "You know barbers do not exist." The barber said, "Well I am here and I am a barber." "No!" the client exclaimed, "They don't exist because if they did there would be no people with long hair and beards like that man who walks in the street."

Moral : It is not necessary to go to God to get His blessings.

21. *Holes in the Fence*

There was a boy who had bad temper. His father gave him a bag of nails and told he must hammer a nail into the back of the fence every time he lost his temper. On the first day, the boy had driven 37 nails into the fence. Soon the number of nails hammered daily gradually dwindled down as he learnt to control his anger. He found easy to control his temper. Finally, the day came when the boy didn't lose his temper. He told his father about it. Now his father told him to pull out one nail for each day that he was able to hold his temper. The day passed and the young boy was finally able to tell his father that all the nails were gone. The father took his son by the hand and led him to the fence and showed the irreparable holes made by the driven nails which looked ugly. Father made him understand, 'When you say things in anger, they leave a scar.'

Moral : We should never say anything in bad temper; it may hurt others.

22. Lesson of Actual Life

Once a boy, with his father was walking on a mountain. The boy inquisitively asked his father many questions about the world. Suddenly, he surprisingly heard a voice repeating, somewhere in the mountain: "AAAhhhhhhhhhhh." Just as he had screamed when he had got injured. He curiously asked, "Who are you?" He received the answer, "Who are you?" and then he screamed to the mountain, "I admire you!" He heard, "I admire you!" Then angrily he screamed, "Coward!"

He received the same. He looked at his father and asked, "What is going on?" Then his father explained, "This is called but really this is life. Our life is simply a reflection of our actions. If you want more love in the world, create more love in your heart. If you want more competence in your team, improve your competence."

Moral : As you sow, so shall you reap.

23. Love for the Mentally Retarded

A few years ago, at the Seattle Special Olympics, nine contestants, all physically or mentally disabled, assembled at the starting line for the 100 metres race. At the fire of the gun, they started with a relish to run the race to the finish and win. One little boy among them stumbled on the asphalt, tumbled and began to cry. The other eight heard the boy crying and slowed down to look back. Rather than winning the race, they all went to soothe him. One girl with Down's syndrome bent down and kissed him and said, "This will make it better." Then all nine linked arms and walked together to the finish line. Everyone in the stadium applauded for them that gave them real triumph. Thus they set an example for all who were present there.

Moral : To please your surroundings is never less than to get the trophy in a race, even if you slow down in real competitions.

24. The Precious Gift

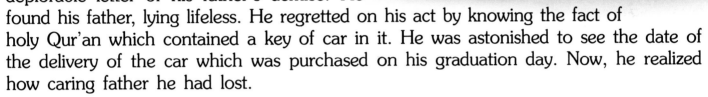

Once a young boy was going to get a graduation degree. For many months he had been admiring a beautiful sports car in a dealer's showroom. Knowing his father could well afford it, he told him that was all he wanted. He was sure that he would have that car as a gift from his father. On the morning of his graduation his father called him and handed a beautiful wrapped gift box. He inquisitively opened the gift but finding a leather-bound holy Qur'an, he acrimoniously threw that and stormed out of the house. He never contacted his father for many years. But one day, he immediately left for his house after reading a deplorable letter of his father's demise. He found his father, lying lifeless. He regretted on his act by knowing the fact of holy Qur'an which contained a key of car in it. He was astonished to see the date of the delivery of the car which was purchased on his graduation day. Now, he realized how caring father he had lost.

Moral : Always respect your parents' decision.

25. The Ant and the Dove

In a scorching hot day, an ant was walking around in search of water. After sometime she reached a spring where she had to climb up a blade of grass. She slipped and fell into the water while making her way up. She could have been drowned if a dove up

a nearby tree had not seen her. Seeing the ant in trouble the dove quickly dropped a leaf into the water near the struggling ant. Now the ant was saved which made her indebted to the dove. A profound intimacy developed between them that sustained till end. Time passed happily. One day, a deplorable condition occurred with the arrival of a hunter who had caught that dove but the ant remembered the dove's favour and bit on the heel of the hunter. The inflamed heel made him to drop his net. Now the dove was quick to fly away.

Moral : One good turn is rewarded with another.

26. Two Pots

Once upon a time, there was a man who had two pots. As one was good, it delivered full water in it but another was cracked. For two years, the long walk from the stream to the master's house, the cracked pot arrived only half full. The perfect pot flaunted on its accomplishment but the cracked pot humiliated it for its imperfection. After two years, the cracked pot asked the man in spite of being petty and insignificant, "Why do you carry water in me?" The man didn't reply anything; he just took both pots and showed the way from where he had been taking water for two years. They saw that one side of path was barren but another side was filled with beautiful flowers. Then the man explained, "It was the cracked pot which watered those plants and the flowers blossomed in them." The cracked pot became very happy of its accomplishment.

Moral : A shapeless body can also give shape to others.

27. The Ant and the Grasshopper

One cold, frosty day in the middle of winter, a colony of ants was busy drying out some, grains of corn, which had grown damp during the wet autumn weather.

A half dead grasshopper, with cold and hunger, came up to one of the ants, and begged to give it a piece or two from their store of corn to save its life. The ant said, "We worked day and night to get this corn in. Why should I give it to you?"

"What were you doing all last summer when you should have been gathering your food?"

"Oh, I didn't have time for things like that," said the grasshopper, "I was far too busy singing to carry corn about." The ant laughed unkindly. "In that case you can sing all winter as far as I am concerned," he said. And without another word he turned back to his work.

Moral : We should always be prepared for our future.

28. The Farmer and the Farm-hand

Once a farmer constantly advertised to hire hands for his land, along the seacoast. Most people dreaded the awful storms that raged across the ocean and denied to work on farms. After a steady stream of refusals the farmer met a short thin man, during the interview of the applicants. The farmer asked, "Are you a good farm-hand?" Then the man only replied, "I can sleep when the wind blows." Although puzzled by this answer, the farmer, desperate for help, hired him. The farmer felt satisfied with the man, working from dawn to dusk. One night, hearing a loud howled wind, the farmer jumped from bed, grabbed a lantern and rushed to wake the farm-hand up to tie things down before they blew away. But he didn't move. Acrimoniously, the farmer himself went to tie things. But he was amazed to see everything, in its appropriate position. The farmer then understood the words said by the farm-hand and confidently went to sleep.

Moral : Work done in advance reaps good results.

29. The Fox and the Stork

Once a stork was invited to the dinner by a selfish fox at his home. The stork reached the fox's home and knocked at the door with her long beak. The fox welcomed her with open arms and offered to have dinner together. The fox served soup in shallow bowls for both. As the bowl was too shallow for the stork's beak, she couldn't have any of it but the fox licked up all his soup very quickly. The poor stork went ballistic but remained polite and ravenous.

To show retaliation against the fox, the stork also invited him to the dinner next day. This time again, soup was served, but in tall jugs. The stork devoured the soup easily but the fox couldn't reach inside the tall jug. This time the fox remained famished.

Moral : A selfish act can backfire on you.

30. The Saint's Lesson

A saint was once preaching to his disciples. One of the disciples asked how they could be endowed with the brilliance of creativity. The disciple meant to say–could any task performed by them make sure of their creative sense? Thereupon the saint provided a sieve to his disciples and said to fill water in the sieve. The disciples after making numerous attempts held their heads in despair. They were unsuccessful in completing the task. Then the saint took the sieve and threw it far away in water Gradually, it started sinking and thus the sieve was filled with water.

Moral- A creative mind can solve any puzzle.

31. The Boy and the Berries

Once, a boy was playing near some hedges laden with berries that appeared ripe and juicy. His mouth watered and he licked his chops. Immediately, he started gathering the berries. Just then, he got stung sharply by a nettle. He started feeling pain and

soon, a rash appeared on his hand. Leaving the collection of berries, he ran home. With tears in his eyes, he told his mother everything. Sobbing hard, he said, "Mom! I touched them lightly but they stung me hard." The mother smiled and caressing her son, replied, "They stung you because you touched them lightly. Had you held them firmly, they wouldn't have hurt you. You can't get anything without facing dangers. Every rose has some thorns to protect it. So, if you want berries, learn to grasp the nettles."

Moral : Never lose heart in adverse circumstances.

32. The Shepherd's Proposal

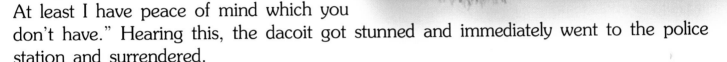

One cold morning, a poor shepherd was grazing his cattle in a pasture. He had neither enough clothes to wear nor even a pair of shoes. Suddenly, a man came there on a horse, a notorious dacoit. He dismounted, went to the shepherd and said, "Come and work with me. I will give you clothes and shoes." But the shepherd denied going with the dacoit. Hearing this the dacoit was baffled and started to beat him. Again, the dacoit said to him, "You will not have to worry even for your food." At this the shepherd replied, "In spite of doing a very simple work, I can manage two loaves of bread for myself. I am content being a shepherd. At least I have peace of mind which you don't have." Hearing this, the dacoit got stunned and immediately went to the police station and surrendered.

Moral : Peace of mind is more necessary than luxury of life.

33. The Diamond Necklace

A king, once presented his daughter an engagingly beautiful diamond necklace. She loved the gift and kept it in her room. But somehow it went missing that made the king and the princess perplexed. The king then announced to reward of ₹ 50,000 to the one who would return it. All people along with the courtiers searched for the necklace but couldn't find it. A few days passed; a tailor saw the necklace

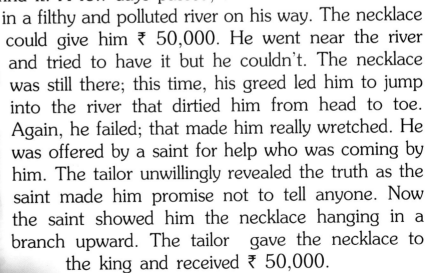

in a filthy and polluted river on his way. The necklace could give him ₹ 50,000. He went near the river and tried to have it but he couldn't. The necklace was still there; this time, his greed led him to jump into the river that dirtied him from head to toe. Again, he failed; that made him really wretched. He was offered by a saint for help who was coming by him. The tailor unwillingly revealed the truth as the saint made him promise not to tell anyone. Now the saint showed him the necklace hanging in a branch upward. The tailor gave the necklace to the king and received ₹ 50,000.

Moral : Surrounding knowledge also produces result.

34. United we Stand, Divided we Fall

A father had a family of sons who were perpetually quarreling among themselves. When he failed to heal their disputes by his exhortations, he determined to give them a practical illustration of the evils of disunion. For this purpose he one day told them to bring a bundle of sticks. When they had done so, he placed the faggot into the hands of each of them in succession, and ordered them to break it into pieces. They tried with all their strength, and were not able to do it. Next, he opened the faggot, took the sticks separately, one by one, and again put them into his sons' hands, which they broke easily. He then addressed them in these words, "My sons, if you are of one mind, and unite to assist one an other, you will be as this faggot, uninjured by all the attempts of your enemies; but if you are divided among yourselves, you will be broken as easily as these sticks."

Moral : There is strength in unity.

35. The Man and the Cocoon of Butterfly

Once a man saw a small opening appeared on the cocoon of a butterfly. He sat and watched the butterfly for several hours as it struggled to force its body through that little hole. Then it seemed to stop making any progress. It appeared as if it had made as far as it could and it could go no farther. Then the man decided to help the butterfly, so he took a pair of scissors and snipped off the remaining bit of the cocoon. The butterfly then emerged easily. But it had a swollen body and small, shrivelled wings. The man had thought to help it and expected to be everything good but the butterfly spent the rest of its life crawling around with a swollen body and shrivelled wings. It could never fly. Actually, he benignly opened the path of progress, but restricted Nature's process for the cocoon to struggle.

Moral : Struggle nurtures our efficiency and potentials.

36. The Merchant and his Foolish Donkey

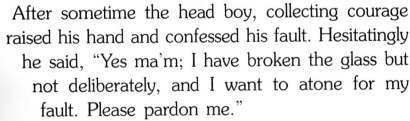

One beautiful spring morning, a merchant loaded his donkey with the bags of salt to go to the market in order to sell them. The merchant and his donkey were walking along together. They had not walked far when they reached a river on the road. Unfortunately, the donkey slipped and fell into the river and noticed that the bags of salt loaded on his back became lighter. There was nothing the merchant could do, except return home where he loaded his donkey with more bags of salt. As they reached the slippery riverbank, now deliberately, the donkey fell into the river and wasted all the bags of salt on its back again. The merchant quickly discovered the donkey's trick. He then returned home again but re-loaded his donkey with the bags of sponges. The foolish, tricky donkey again set on its way. On reaching the river he again fell into the water. But instead of the load becoming lighter, it became heavier.

Moral : We should not pretend. Cunning nature can harm you.

37. The Teacher and the Boy

"Who did it," a teacher was asking the class again and again. But she couldn't get the answer. The teacher again asked, "Who did it?" Covering some steps again she got nothing.

After sometime the head boy, collecting courage raised his hand and confessed his fault. Hesitatingly he said, "Yes ma'm; I have broken the glass but not deliberately, and I want to atone for my fault. Please pardon me."

By hearing this the teacher didn't say anything. She went to the library and bought a book, and gave to the boy by saying, "I am giving you this book as reward not for breaking the glass but for accepting your fault. And I am glad to see that my labour of nurturing good habits in you has worked."

Moral : Honesty can reform the mistake.

38. The Casket with Gems

In village Rampur, a decrepit lady lamented his dead husband. In the beginning, her two sons showed compassion for her but soon got disenchanted with their mother. Now the pathetic condition of her life made her to go to her friend Sheela, whom she related all her problems of not even getting proper diet in her own house. The shrewd woman wilfully showed her a way by which she would be dominating in her house and gave her a mysterious casket, full of gems. When the widow reached her house, she was given more attention. Both her sons asked about the casket, in her hand. She replied that the casket was given by her husband in his declining days. It was filled with precious stone and gems. Now their avarice for the casket made them too caring for the lady. In due course, they used to ask for the key of the casket but she ignored by saying that it must be given to them. One day, the lady was grappled with a disease and died. After funeral, the sons broke the casket and found it filled with stones, gravel, etc.

Moral : Greed gives nothing.

39. Cats and Roosters

Long, long ago, in Africa cats were ruled by roosters where cats had to collect food for the king roosters for the sake of their life. If someone dared to disobey the king, he would have given an iron comb's burn as a punishment. So all cats were petrified of the hot comb. All cats had to work hard for gathering food. One day Mrs. Cat got a chance to enter and observe the gigantic home of king rooster when he was found fast asleep. Mrs. Cat wanted to know the secret of the hotness of that comb, so she touched it timidly. She was astounded to feel it because it was of normal temperature. Now she understood the trick of roosters. No longer afraid, the cats pervaded there. All the cooks ran away to see the cats.

Moral : Tricks never persist for long.

40. Cause of Grief

Once there lived a rich man with his loyal servant. The man was always rejoiced because of the loyal and meticulous attitude of his servant. One evening, the man was shocked to see the broken watch of his room. He called his servant and angrily asked the reason for that. The servant replied that in order to clean the room, the watch inadvertently slipped from his hands and parted in many pieces. The man loved him so much that, he could not scold him. Morning passed but night was impassable for the merchant. His penchant for that watch led him not to sleep but the servant had a sound sleep, which made the man infuriated. Next day, the man told the servant that he was so wretched because the very watch he wanted to gift him for his diligence but unfortunately, it was broken by him. Had it been safe, it would have been his. This statement now led the servant not to sleep and the man was now in great succour.

Moral : Tension for possession causes grief.

41. Cherries in Mud

One day, while walking down the road, father said to his son, "Look, a horseshoe is lying in the mud. Pick it up." The son said, "I hate to pick up things from mud." The father picked up the horseshoe and kept it in his pocket. On reaching the village, he sold the horseshoe and bought some cherries. Father understood the desire of his son and dropped a cherry on the ground. The son picked it up, washed it and ate it up. Then father said to him, "Sometimes even small things cost much. These cherries are here because of that horseshoe that you refused to pick up from the mud." The son understood what his father meant.

Moral : Little things cost much.

42. The Cloud and the Farmer

Once a saint predicted that it would not rain for seven years. When a simple farmer heard this news, he took his plough and kept in home and thought if it would not rain for seven years, then it's not necessary to irrigate the field. He sat three days at home with no work but on the fourth day he felt bored. He thought, 'If I would not irrigate the field, I will forget the use of plough.' Thinking this he took his plough and went to irrigate his field. Now he was happy that he would practise irrigation in spite of no rain. Then he saw a cloud while working, but he didn't like to see it. Suddenly, the cloud called the farmer and said, "O foolish farmer, it has been predicted that it would not rain for seven years. Why are you wasting your time in the field? We would not come as rain." Then the farmer replied that he was baffled to think that if he would not use the plough in irrigation, he might forget the use. Hearing this, the cloud thought, 'That the farmer is right; if I would also not go as rain on earth, I can also forget my work.' From that day on, it started raining.

Moral : We should never lose hope.

43. The Cows and the Lion

In a green and fresh pasture, there lived three cows, a white, a black and a brown cow. They were kind to one another and always grazed together. One day, a ravenous lion came to devour them all but couldn't, because of their company. But the lion made a policy of divide and rule and visited them. He said that he remembered them a lot to know about their health. The brown cow, being so gentle was entangled in his trap and accepted the lion's friendship. Next day, the lion secretly called the brown cow and said that the colour of his body was dark like the black cow but the white cow didn't match with them. So it was better to kill him. The brown cow agreed and kept the black cow immersed in gossips. Meanwhile, the lion killed the white cow. After a few days, the lion attacked and demolished the black cow. A few days later, the lion killed the brown cow and ate her mercilessly.

Moral : Never cheat good friends.

44. The Dacoit and the Fish

Once upon a time in Arabian city an atrocious dacoit lived with his enormous soldiers. A deplorable atmosphere pervaded with his presence when he used to pass any village of Arabian city because he brutally snatched all the valuable things along with money from villagers. He committed such crimes daily but at the end of the day he daily used to go to a pond near by his castle and gave the loaves of bread to fish. One day, he got an injury which led to his death. Now his soul was being taken to hell for his merciless acts. Suddenly, an angel of God said, "No matter he made villagers' life terrible but on the other hand, he has fed the fish. So he must be given more life for living." After that he left his devastating acts forever.

Moral : Sin can be pulverized by humanity and nobility.

45. The Diamond Stone

Once in a forest, a washerman was going with his donkey hanging a stone in his neck. A jeweller on his way got his eyes on the stone. He recognized the stone as a diamond but the washerman, not acquainted with this fact, got surprised to know that the jeweller wanted to buy the stone. The washerman demanded one rupee for the stone. But the jeweller refused and went ahead. Again, the washerman met another jeweller who also recognized the stone to be a diamond and showed his intention to buy it.

The amazed washerman priced it ₹ 2; the second jeweller nodded his head and gave him two rupees for the stone and took it. Meanwhile, the first jeweller came back to him panting heavily and offered one rupee for the stone but soon turned pale to know that the stone had already been sold.

Then he revealed that the ordinary stone was actually a diamond and addressed the washerman foolish. Thereupon, the washerman said, "You are more foolish than I."

Moral : Opportunities seldom come.

46. *Distance*

Once upon a time, it rained heavily for several days resulting in floods. Many houses collapsed and household articles got carried away with the flood-water. As a matter of chance, two pitchers were also carried away by the flowing tide. One of them was made of brass while the other of baked clay. The brass pitcher was so strong, that, it could be tossed against anything. But the clay pitcher was in ever-present danger of being broken if it got struck against something. The clay pitcher was alarmed by danger. The brass pitcher looked at it and said, "Brother! Be close to me; I shall protect you in every way." The clay pitcher thought wisely and retorted, "Brother! It would surely be worse for me, if we come closer. If I keep at a distance from you, I may float to safety." So, the clay pitcher stood away from the brass pitcher and safely reached the shore.

Moral : Little distance enhances love.

47. *Effect of Voice*

Once a guru went to a forest in search of remedy. A hunter had also gone there for hunting animals and a solider also arrived there. All of three felt thirsty. They saw a hut in the forest in which a blind man was sitting. The hunter went there and said, "O blind man, make me drink water; otherwise, your pot of water would be broken by me." The blind man didn't give water to him and moved him away. Then the soldier came to him and said, "O blind man, give me water and take anything you want." Hearing this the man got angry and moved him away as well. The guru went to the blind man and addressed him politely and very humbly asked for water. Hearing a very gentle voice the man said, "I have become satisfied that you arrived in my hut; take and drink water." After drinking water the guru told, "When a hunter and a soldier came and asked water, you denied. But when I came and asked water, you gave water. Why is it so?" Then the blind man replied that it all depended upon the voice of a person.

Moral : Voice should be humble and gentle.

48. Family

A cute son was desperately waiting for his dad, who got late from office and was exasperated due to some problem. No sooner had he opened the door for his dad than he started showering questions about his income. It infuriated father much more and he replied it was none of his business but again, the child asked how much money he made in an hour. Father angrily replied $20. The son now demanded for his one hour earning, $20. Father said, "You are brought every toy and chocolate you need. How dare you ask me for money?" He rebuked him. He soon realized his mistake of being harsh to his delicate child. So he gave him $10, but the child had already $10. Again, that agitated father, but the son soothingly pacified him by saying, "Here is $20; now can I buy an hour of your time? Please come home early tomorrow so that we may have dinner with you."

Moral : Spending time with family enhances love.

49. The Farmer's Cat

A farmer had some cats to sell. He was hanging a board for advertisement. There came a little boy to buy a cat but was avoided by saying that the cost of cats was too exorbitant to afford for him. The boy delved hard into his pocket to take out the money and gave it to the farmer. The farmer took the boy to a room where all the cats were kept. The boy was given a beautiful cat, but soon the boy noticed a disabled cat and decided to choose that cat. On asking that why he chose that cat, he replied, "You see sir, I don't run too well myself, and he will need someone who can understand him."

Moral : The world is full of people who need someone who understands.

50. God's Company

Once two friends were passing through a forest. Now it was time of Namaz. So they both decided to offer Namaz. When both were busy in prayers, they heard the roar of a lion. The first friend got frightened and climbed on a tree but the second friend kept praying. The lion came there and gazed at him and the first friend but didn't do anything and went from there. Then both friends went ahead. Suddenly, the second friend slapped himself on his cheek in order to kill a mosquito. Then the first friend observed that when a lion had come during prayers, he didn't move but now he got scared of a small mosquito. Then the second friend replied, "That time I was with God and now I am with a person."

Moral : God's company always makes fearless.

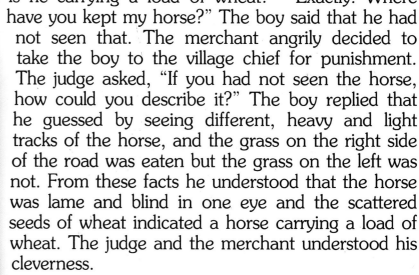

51. The Wise Boy and the Merchant

Once a merchant with his horse carrying two sacks of wheat was on his way to the market. Meanwhile, the merchant got exhausted and decided to take a nap. When he woke up, he didn't find his horse and started searching for it everywhere. On the way he met a boy. He asked the boy about the horse. The boy asked, "Is the horse's left eye blind, his right foot lame and is he carrying a load of wheat?" "Exactly. Where have you kept my horse?" The boy said that he had not seen that. The merchant angrily decided to take the boy to the village chief for punishment. The judge asked, "If you had not seen the horse, how could you describe it?" The boy replied that he guessed by seeing different, heavy and light tracks of the horse, and the grass on the right side of the road was eaten but the grass on the left was not. From these facts he understood that the horse was lame and blind in one eye and the scattered seeds of wheat indicated a horse carrying a load of wheat. The judge and the merchant understood his cleverness.

Moral : One should not be quick in judging people.

52. True Friendship

Two very fast friends were really dejected, because of exploitation by their cruel king. One of the friends decided to raise his voice against the king. When the king came to know this, he sentenced the boy to death. Before hanging, the boy expressed a wish to meet his family. But the king rejected the request. Seeing this the other friend again requested the king to permit his friend to go his family and also added he should be hanged, in case his friend did not return. The king accepted his condition and gave six days' ultimatum to come back. Till then his friend was kept in observation as prisoner. Six days passed; he didn't return. So his friend was to be hanged. But at the eleventh hour he came and said to hang him. But his friend offered him to go back to his family and was ready to be hanged. Long arguments between them for each other's life were really poignant. It shed tears from the king's eyes, and the king decided to appoint them court advisers.

Moral : Tenderness makes progress.

53. The Man in Forest

A man was being chased by a hungry lion. To save his life, the man climbed on a tree where he sat on a branch. But two rats, black and white, were cutting the same branch. To escape from the fate, he decided to jump on the other branch. He turned pale to see a boa, opening his mouth to engulf the man. Now he was really out of wits. To get out of these he looked upward where there was a honeycomb. As he tried to touch it, he was lost in amazing taste of honey drops, that fell on his mouth. He again got another drop of honey which was enough to forget all his foes, viz lion, rats, boa. Suddenly, he realized it was nothing but the trick of his son to wake him up. Actually, he was in a dream. He decided to go to decipher the message of the dream. It was explained that the lion is your death; it keeps chasing you. Rats are day and night. With the passage of time they make you close to death; the boa is your grave. It is always wanting you to fall into it. The honeycomb is the world, and honey is the luxury of life which help us to forget our death, grave and inevitable things.

Moral : Luxury diverts our mind.

54. The Peacock and the Crane

Once a peacock was dancing in a forest spreading his feathers out. No doubt, he looked very beautiful and felt proud of his feathers. Suddenly, a crane came there. He wished the peacock and they started talking. While talking, the peacock looked at the feathers of the crane with hatred. The crane asked the peacock, "Why are you looking at me like this?" The peacock replied, "I am looking at your dull feathers; they have no lustre and beauty. See mine; how attractive they are! Nature has done so much injustice to you- such a strong bird and so dull feathers. This is really a pity." The crane replied, "Nature has always been fair with every creature. Though you have beautiful feathers while mine are dull, yet I can fly high in the clouds and you can't do that at all." The peacock felt ashamed and begged the crane's pardon.

Moral : We should not criticize anybody's appearance.

55. Heaven and Hell

Once a rich merchant died of a severe disease. He used to oppress the people. He was drawn by an angel to heaven. He found the place rather calm with clement weather but the monotonous merchant felt weird to find no newspaper, no hustle-bustle of market and hotel. He then requested the angel to take him to hell, where he found everything, he missed in paradise. There was chaos all around. People were making fuss and pandemonium. All these things enthralled the merchant very much and he decided to stay there. So the angel left him in hell. As soon as the angel vanished, the door of hell was shut. All dwellers started behaving outrageously and pouncing upon him. He was taken to hot oil to fry and to burn. He was really petrified of these but could not avoid and get rid of what was going with him.

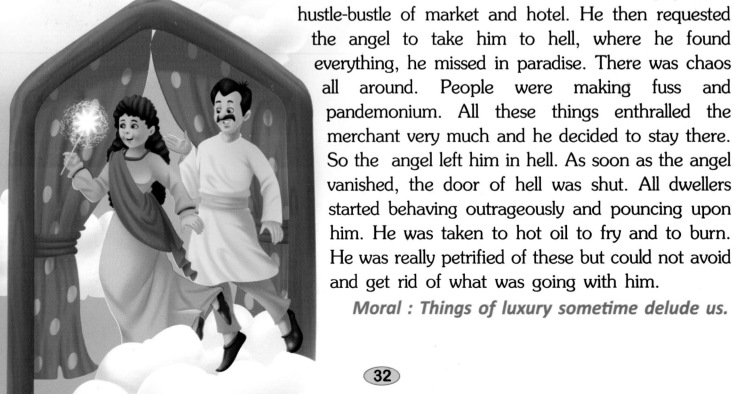

Moral : Things of luxury sometime delude us.

56. The King and the Old Woman

Once a king desired anyone who had seen God in his lifetime be brought before him. After some time a very old woman was brought before the king. The king asked her, "Did you see God yourself?" She said, "Yes." Then the king asked her if she remembered any narration from Him. Then she replied, "When old age comes two things become young-one is hope and the other is greed." The king thanked her and gave her one hundred dinars. The woman thanked the king and went away. Half the way some thought passed through her mind and she desired to be brought before the king once more. When again she was brought, the king asked, "Why did you come back?" She said, "I just came to inquire whether the monies you gave me were once for all or is it to continue every year?" The king thought, 'How true God's words are!' She had hope of life even now and she had greed for money too. The king said, "Don't worry; you will be paid every year." She was taken a back but on the way she breathed her last.

Moral : *Too much greed leads to one's downfall.*

57. Hunger for Gold

Sikandar was a dominant emperor. He wanted to win the whole world. To fulfil his wish he proceeded with his soldiers and crushed many cities. He attacked a city. Once he stopped his horse and knocked at a door of a house. But nobody came. After knocking again an old lady came. Sikander rudely asked for some bread. The lady recognized him as Sikander. She went inside and brought a casket filled with jewels. Sikander acrimoniously said, "What is this? I had asked for some bread but what you have brought." "Jewels." The lady seriously said, "I know you are Sikander. Your hunger is not for bread, but for gold. If your hunger had been for bread, you wouldn't have been here to snatch other's bread." These words made him to think again and again and his pride was shattered. After that, he begged her pardon, and went from that city without taking anything.

Moral : *Pride hath a fall.*

58. Mutual Understanding

Once a Guru decided to give test to his disciples. So he called his 20 disciples for having meals. The Guru divided them in two groups of 10 boys each. He served them food but before eating he kept a condition. Without bending their elbows they would have to eat. Both groups got confused. Both groups tried a lot to eat without bending their elbows but couldn't. Food got scattered hither and thither. The first group of boys kept trying, but after a short discussion the second group got an idea. They started to feed one another without bending their elbows and completed their task. The Guru became happy to see that his disciples had passed the test and became aware that mutual understanding among a group can solve the toughest of the tasks of the life.

Moral : Through mutual understanding even the toughest task can be solved.

59. Miracle of Meditation

Once a man killed a person. So the soldiers of that kingdom were told to catch him by the king. He kept running in order to save his life from the soldiers. Then he reached near a river, but he found difficult to cross the river, and he didn't want to be caught as well. Then he saw a saint applying ash on his body, sitting riverside. He was busy in meditation. The culprit also decided to sit, applying ash on his body. He was enjoying that moment. The soldiers of the king reached there, chasing him. When they saw saints sitting there, they touched their feet. Seeing this, the culprit was astonished, "I am only a fake saint but what they felt, they touched my feet." Then he thought if untruth was such powerful, then truth must be super powerful. Touching their feet the soldiers went from there, but from that day on the killer totally changed himself and gave up bad deeds.

Moral : Truth is more powerful than untruth.

60. Path of Salvation

Once prince Siddhartha was wandering in a garden. Meanwhile, he saw a shepherd driving 10-11 sheep and goats. The prince asked the shepherd where he was taking all animals cruelly. The shepherd replied that all these animals were being taken for sacrifice in a special ceremony of king Bindsar. The prince followed the shepherd to the place where worship was going to be held. After sometime prince Siddhartha reached that place and resisted king Bindsar by adding the fact of life. He said, "Animals are also like humans; they have their families. Then why do we take their life for our purposes? Killing animals never give us salvation. It gives us a kind of unsatisfaction. So we should stop doing all these things and never imprison animals."

Moral : Don't hurt others for own purpose.

61. The Peacock's Ugly Voice

It was a fine day during the rainy season. A peacock was dancing happily in a forest. Suddenly, he was reminded of his ugly rough voice. His face turned pale and his eyes started watering. Suddenly, he saw a nightingale sitting on a nearby tree and singing. Listening to her voice, the peacock lamented, "What a sweet voice she has! Everybody praises but when I utter a sound, everybody makes fun of me. How jinxed I am!" Just then, there appeared, the goddess. She asked the peacock, "Why are you sad?" The peacock sobbed out, "I have got such a beautiful body that is praised by all but my voice is so bad that everyone laughs at it. So this beauty is useless." The goddess replied, "You are the only one who is unhappy. Several creatures have been gifted by God with various gifts like- you the beauty, eagle the strength, nightingale the sweet voice, so on and so forth. So don't grumble over your weakness; accept the way it is and be happy."

Moral : One should not regret on what one doesn't have. Rather, be satisfied with what we have.

62. Realisation of Mistake

A deer and a doe lived happily in the forest. Once a big confrontation occurred. One day, the doe left her abode and went to a nearby jungle and started staying with another deer. They enjoyed their life. When they both were resting in a cave, they heard the roar of a lion. The doe said to the deer, "What shall we do now? This lion will kill us both." The deer replied, "I am going my way. You take care of yourself." The doe was taken aback. She recalled how her husband saved her many times from crisis. She fled from the back of the cave and soon reached her husband. The deer felt very happy to see his wife back. The doe realized her mistake and promised to behave well.

Moral : Never get annoyed with the one who loves you.

63. Religion or Wealth

Once a saint lived in a distant isolated hut. Yet, people went to him to get panacea for their problems. One day, an enormously wealthy man decided to go there and inquire about religion in the world. He asked, "Life can't run without money, so wealth should be given more priority than religion." Then the man spent a whole day with the saint. When darkness fell, the saint lit a lamp, but its light disturbed the man to take a sound sleep. The man asked, "For how long will it light up?" The saint replied, "Till there is darkness." Lastly, the saint added, "Light covers darkness, in the same way religion triumphs over sin."

Moral : Religion is a part and parcel of life.

64. The Rose and the Lily

Once there was a gardener having a beautiful garden of flower-plants-mostly rose plants. By chance a lily plant blossomed near a rose-bush. A lily plant is believed to yield flowers that never fade and have an everlasting beauty. But the rose flowers have a short life. The lily said to the rose, "How beautiful you are! What an aroma you possess! No wonder, you are universally a favourite flower. I really envy you." The rose replied, "You wouldn't have said so, if you had known the reality. My bloom is very short-lived. I bloom in the morning and by sunset I begin to lose shine. By the next morning I fade completely and then I die. But you are known to have flowers that never fade even if they have been cut. Beauty is only a nine-day wonder."

Moral : Eternal beauty is more necessary than outer beauty.

65. In Search of Peace

Once, a king decided to give his kingdom's biggest prize to a boy for his bravery. But the boy was not happy with this. When the king came to know, he himself went to the boy and said him to ask for anything as a reward. But the boy again denied taking anything. When the king asked him what the reason behind it, the boy replied that he wanted only peace of mind as a reward. He wanted neither money nor reward. Then the king decided to take the boy to a saint who himself was so peaceful and would be able to provide him with peace. When the king told him that the boy wanted only peace as a reward then the saint replied that he himself was not peaceful; how could he give him peace? Peace is that wealth which can't be given or taken by others.

Moral : Peace of mind is the biggest wealth.

66. Secret of Light

This is the story of that epoch when there was no entity of light, so people were anxious to bring the light in villages because darkness made their life gloomy. So they had decided to throw one basket of darkness daily. This custom continued for long. In that village, a man named Ashish lived; he did not like this job. So he went to the other village and married a girl named Rupvati. When they both returned to that village, the bride was given a work of throwing darkness in a far pit, before entering the house. She was amazed and thought deeply. Soon she tore the edge of her sari, took an earthen pot and kerosene. By striking two stones she lit the earthen pot. Then the whole village was filled with effulgence which made all villagers ecstatic.

Moral : Knowledge works wonder.

67. The Selfish Dove

Once in a country, a very devastating famine occurred which caused many creatures to die before time. There lived a group of doves. The oldest dove said to them to move towards a mountainous place, where they could at least have little grains. But they found nothing. Among them there was a greedy dove, who only wanted to mitigate his pang of hunger. So he ventured to the bottom of the mountain in search of grains. He secretly went to have that. Fortunately, he saw many carts full of crops with holes in it. The roads were littered with seeds that he could eat. The same thing continued for many days. One day, he was eating the crop but engrossed in his profit only. He could not notice the coming cart and was crushed as wheat in machine. He died and the flying old dove saw his tattered body. The old dove took no time to understand everything.

Moral : Selfishness brings mishap.

68. The Foolish Bear

Once there was a ravenous bear that went riverside in search of food. He started searching for fish into the water. He saw a fish and pounced on it but soon left the fish thinking, that it's too small to fill his stomach. Then he caught another fish and found it too small, so he again left it. This way, he caught many small fish, still thinking that the small fish would not fill his belly. By sunset the bear could not catch any big fish. He became tired having kept standing for very long. He now felt sorry for having let off so many fish. He realized that all those small fish together would have filled up his belly, but now it was too late. He had to remain hungry that day.

Moral : Greed may not finish your hunger.

69. The King and God

There was a kind-hearted and generous king. Once there spread famine in his kingdom. There remained nothing to eat, so the king ordered to open the godown of the grains of his kingdom so that poor people might also get benefited and eat the food of the kitchen of his palace. Finally, that time when nothing remained to eat for the king's family even, a stranger appeared with a big bowl filled with kheer made of milk, sugar and rice, in front of the king. The king first of all made his servants to eat. His all servants and family member ate the kheer. Nothing remained for the king. Then God appeared and said, "I am impressed with your benevolence; ask for something you need." Then the king fell at God's feet and said, "I don't want anything but a heart filled with kindness which can feel the pain of others."

Moral : Kindness can let you meet God.

70. A Life of Satisfaction

Once a fisherman was reclining against the dock with a few fish in his bucket. A rich merchant was passing over there and noticed him. He asked, "Why are you squandering your time in rest? Go and trap some more fish." The fisherman replied, "I have caught all I need for today and I am smoking my pipe to enjoy the breeze." The businessman objected, "If you will use time in fishing, you could earn more money than requirement." The fisherman replied, "And then what." "Well, then your saving would allow you to buy a bigger boat so that you may go farther into the sea to catch bigger fish to make even more money." The businessman replied, "And then what?" "Then you could buy a whole fleet of boats and catch a thousand of fish and make a thousand of rupees in one day and become rich like me." "And then what?" asked the fisherman. "Then you could sit back and enjoy life like I do," the rich man said. "Well, isn't that what I am doing already," said the fisherman proudly.

Moral : A contented man lives life happily.

71. The Monkey and Two Cats

Once upon a time, two cats found a piece of bread and cut it into two pieces. But one piece was slightly bigger than the other. Both the cats wanted the bigger piece. Then they went to a monkey, who was taking a rest in the branch of a tree. They asked him to sort out the matter. The monkey said, "Don't worry. I'll make both the pieces equal." Then it took a bite from the bigger piece. But this made the other piece larger. So it took a bite from the other piece. This continued till the pieces became very small. Seeing this, the cats pleaded, "Sir! We are satisfied. Let us have the pieces now." The shrewd monkey replied, "This is my fee for sorting out the problem." Saying this, it gobbled up the remaining bread. Two cats only kept looking at the face of each other.

Moral : Don't believe in a shrewd judge.

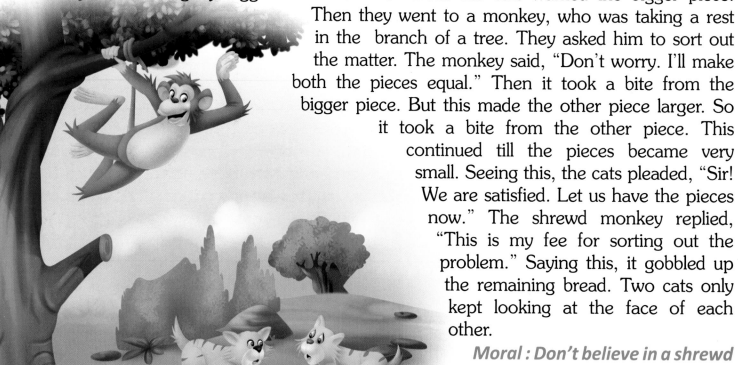

72. The Monkey without a Tail

Once a monkey was wandering in a forest searching for food. As to his bad luck, he got caught up in a trap. He tried his best to get free but lost his tail in the struggle. He felt very small, thinking that now every monkey would laugh at him. He felt so sad that he thought of committing suicide. But then he said to himself, "It is cowardice to kill oneself. I should think of something else." At last, the monkey planned to persuade all the monkeys to part with their tails. So, he called a meeting of all the monkeys and said, "We should get rid of our tails as they are heavy, ugly and tiresome." Though he tried to divert the attention of all the monkeys from his tailless appearance yet one clever monkey noticed it and said, "Sir! You wouldn't have given us this advice, if you weren't tailless. Isn't it?"

Moral : Cleverness escapes you from misfortunes.

73. The Mouse and the Lion

In a hot summer day, a lion was sitting under the shade of a big tree. After some time he fell asleep. Near by, there was a hole, in which there lived a mouse. When the lion was sleeping, the mouse came out of its hole. Unaware of the lion's strength it thought of waking the lion up by running over his body just for fun. Unfortunately, the lion seized it in his strong paw. He was going to kill it when it begged, "Spare me; someday I may repay your mercy." The lion was amused hearing its words and let it go with a smile thinking how such a small mouse could help him. But a day came, when the lion got into trouble. He got caught in a hunter's net under that very tree. As a result, he started roaring loudly. On hearing his roar, the mouse came out of its hole. This was the time to pay back the lion's mercy. So, immediately it along with the other mice nibbled the cords of the net and set the lion free.

Moral : Mercy never goes unrewarded.

74. The Wife and the Husband

Once a wife and her husband were going to their village sitting on a horse. On the way, many people looked at them and said, "Both of them are sitting on a weak horse." To hear this the wife jumped off the horse. As they moved, they met many people who said, "Look at the husband; he is sitting on a horse and his flower-like wife is on foot." Hearing this the husband also jumped off the horse and made his wife to sit on the horse. When people saw this, they again said, "How is she? She is on the horse but her husband is on foot." Now both started to walk on foot. When people saw this, they said, "How foolish both are! In spite of having a horse, both are walking on foot." Both the husband and the wife felt embarrassed and thinking on this matter decided not to hear others and sat on the horse and moved ahead.

Moral : People always say different things; we shouldn't follow them.

75. Always be Thankful to God

Arthur Ashe, the legendary Wimbledon player, was dying of AIDS. From the world over, he received letters from his fans. One of them dolefully asked, "Why does God have chosen you for such a dire or egregious disease?"

To this Arthur Ashe replied, "The world over 5 crore children start playing tennis, 50 lakh learn to play tennis, 5 lakh learn professional tennis, 50,000 come to the circuit, 5000 reach the grand slam, 50 reach Wimbledon, 4 to semi-finals, 2 to the finals. When I was holding a cup I never asked God 'Why me?' And today in pain I should not be asking God, 'Why me?'"

Moral : Be thankful to God for 98% of good things in life.

76. The Unsatisfied Cat

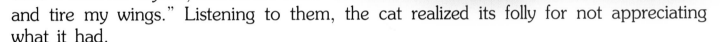

Once a cat was relaxing in a garden when it saw a dog, playing freely. It thought, 'It must be so nice to be play freely.' This feeling of envy made it so bad-tempered, that it didn't even wag its tail at its master, who came to give it some milk. Then it saw a goldfish in the river and wished that it too could live in the cold water. Envy made it angry once again. Just then, it heard the fish say, "It looks so nice and warm on the grass. I wish I could lie down on it." After some time, a sparrow flew past. Seeing the dog lazing around, it said aloud, "I wish I could play the whole day like this cat. I wish I didn't have to build a nest for myself, search for food and tire my wings." Listening to them, the cat realized its folly for not appreciating what it had.

Moral : Be happy with what you have.

77. The Astronomer and the Stranger

Once there lived an astronomer in a town. As we know that astronomers are sky-watchers, he used to go out at night in the open and watch the stars. One night, he was gazing at the sky closely and the same time moving ahead. He got so much involved in sky-watching that he stumbled against the edge of a dry well and fell into it. He laid there groaning in pain. A man passing by heard his groans and came to the well. He asked the astronomer how he got there. The astronomer told him all that happened. The man said, "So you were busy looking into the sky without caring where your feet were carrying you on the ground." "Exactly sir," retorted the astronomer. "Then you deserve it. Helping you would be a folly." Saying this, the man went away.

Moral : Look ahead before you move.

78. Two Cockroaches

Once, two cockroaches, which were young and ful l of energy, lived in a house and played with each other. Both were energetic and strong but there was a difference between them. One cockroach was optimistic and always lived in hope, while the other was pessimistic and lived in despair. One day, they fell into a pot of milk. They swam and tried to hop out, but, as there was no solid support under their feet, it was not possible for the cockroaches to hop out from the pot. After some struggle, the pessimistic cockroach was drowned. On the other hand, the optimistic cockroach kept on struggling, saying to itself, "It seems difficult but who knows! Maybe some miracle will occur. If I try a little longer, something good might happen." Soon the cockroach was able to climb up the heap of butter and hopped out of the pot. Positive thinking had saved the life of the cockroach.

Moral : Nothing is impossible as long as you don't give up.

79. The Best Engineer

There lived a good engineer who was so proud of his work. Once he went to a village for some work, passing many villages and fields. On his way he saw a creeper of pumpkin carried with many pumpkins. After going ahead he saw a big banyan tree, on which many small fruits were there. Seeing this he became surprised and mockingly said how amazing God's creation was. A weak creeper was carrying big pumpkins and a big tree was carrying only small fruits. He went from there. After completing his work when he again returned, he felt exhausted. So he decided to take a nap under a banyan tree's shade. When he woke up, he saw many small fruits around himself. Now he mockingly laughed at himself, "If the banyan tree had fruits as big as pumpkins and they had fallen on his head he would have died." Now he understood that God is the best engineer.

Moral : Mysterious are the ways of God.

80. The Birds and the Beast

Once there broke a war between the birds and the beasts. Many battles were fought one after the other. Sometimes the birds got the upper hand; the next time the beasts were successful. The bats played a very treacherous role in this war. They sided with the side which got the better of the other. Thus they were changing their loyalty from side to side. Neither side paid any attention to the bats till the war lasted. But when the war got over, the bats didn't know which side to go. First, they went to the birds. But the birds refused to own them as many birds had seen them fighting for the beasts. Then, the bats went to the beasts. But there also, they faced the same situation. So, they were left all alone because of their disloyalty.

Moral : Learn to fix your loyalty.

81. Blessing or Curse

Once a great saint with his seven disciples visited a village. The denizens of that village gave a warm welcome with profound respect and the villagers took great care of them. After a few days when the saint was departing he said, "I wish your village would destroy soon and all villagers would be separated." This statement made all the disciples astonished. Again the saint arrived at the other village where they had been disgustingly behaved by the villagers. Then the saint said, "May your village flourish and all people live together forever!"

Such type of blessing led the disciples to ask the reason. Then the saint replied, "If the people of good humanity scatter, they will spread morality and peace but evil people should not be scattered in all over the world; otherwise, they will spread only evil."

Moral : Good people efface evil.

82. Bread of Labour

Once, a saint with his two disciples went to a village. The disciples asked the saint who would provide food in the village. Just then, a carpenter named, Kalo, came and invited them in his home. Kalo thought, 'Let them take rest till he earns money for their food.' Kalo went to a rich merchant's home. That day, the merchant had organized a banquet for the whole villagers but Kalo didn't eat. In the evening, Kalo returned home with flour and vegetables from his wage; his wife started cooking. Meanwhile, the servants of the merchant were asked whether all the villagers had eaten or not. Then they came to know that a saint and two disciples were still ravenous and sleeping in Kalo's house. Then the servants offered them meal but the saint also took Kalo's bread to make him feel happy. But just as the saint took a piece of the merchant's bread, it started bleeding from bread. When he took Kalo's bread, it started flowing milk. The astonished merchant asked the reason. Then the saint replied, "It is the bread of labour." Saying so he enjoyed Kalo's meal.

Moral : Labour gives you satisfaction.

83. Generosity

Once Mahatma Gandhi was wandering villages and cities to collect funds for Charkha Sangh. He was addressing a meeting in Orissa (now Odisha). During one of his tours, a doddering and ailing poor old woman in tattered clothing, proceeded to touch Gandhi's feet on the stage. But she was forcely stopped by volunteers. But she fought her way to the place where Gandhiji was sitting. Then from the folds of her sari she brought out a copper coin and placed it at his feet. Gandhiji picked up the copper coin and put it away carefully but the head of Charkha Sangh refused to take that coin as it had no worth. "This copper coin is worth much more than those thousands," Gandhiji said, "If a man has several lakhs and he gives away a thousand or two, it doesn't mean much." But this coin was perhaps all that the poor woman possessed. She gave me all she had. Gandhiji appreciated for her scarifice.

Moral : Generosity is the best policy.

84. *The Hidden Treasure*

Once upon a time there was a very hard-working farmer. He had a field which gave a rich crop of grapes every year. He had three sons but none of them bothered to help their father in his work. They were very easy-going kind of people. So, the farmer was very worried about their future. One day, the farmer fell ill due to old age. He called his son and said, "Dear sons! I doubt my end is near and before dying I want to tell you that, in my grapery, there lies a hidden treasure. Dig it out after my death." Saying this, the old farmer died. After performing the last rituals of their father, the sons began digging the vine-yard. They dug every inch of it but found nothing. But the digging led to such a rich crop as had never been there before even when their father was alive. So, the sons came to know what their father meant by hidden treasure.

Moral : Hard labour is our hidden treasure.

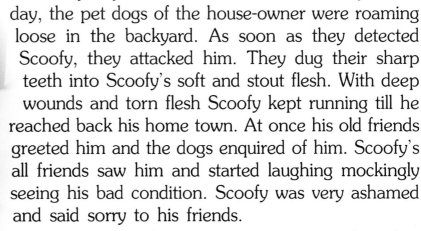

85. *The Insatiable Dog*

Once, a dog named Scoofy lived with his friends in a small town. He ate whatever he wanted to eat and slept in the shade of an oak tree. Though he was enjoying his life in town yet he was not satisfied and always hoped to have something better than what he had. One night, when his all friends were sleeping, he woke up at midnight and without saying anything to his friends he ran away towards the city. In the city he found a house with a place in the back-yard where all waste food was dumped. Scoofy ate the delicious leftovers every day and turned stout in a few days. One day, the pet dogs of the house-owner were roaming loose in the backyard. As soon as they detected Scoofy, they attacked him. They dug their sharp teeth into Scoofy's soft and stout flesh. With deep wounds and torn flesh Scoofy kept running till he reached back his home town. At once his old friends greeted him and the dogs enquired of him. Scoofy's all friends saw him and started laughing mockingly seeing his bad condition. Scoofy was very ashamed and said sorry to his friends.

Moral : Grass always seems greener on the other side of the fence.

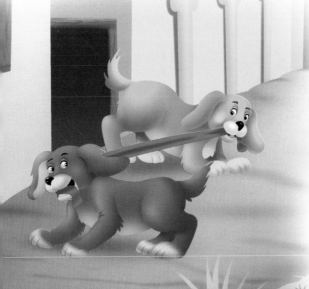

86. *Humiliation*

A lady in a gingham dress and her husband, dressed in a homespun threadbare suit, went to meet the president of Harward university. But they were ignominiously snapped by the secretary, who said, "A meeting of two hours is going on; you can't disturb him during the meeting." They both kept waiting for 2 hours. After sometime the president came and asked their purpose. The man said, "We are parents of that accomplished child who died one year ago. So we want to erect a memorial in his memory." The president denied to give them place in the university. But the lady said, "Is that all it costs to start a university? Why don't we just start our own?" The president's face wilted in confusion and bewilderment. Mr. and Mrs. Leland Stanford got up and went to California where they established the University that bears their name, Stanford University, a memorial to a son that Harvard no longer cared about.

Moral : Don't judge a book by its cover.

87. *Illusion*

Once, a saint called his disciple with whom the saint was very enchanted. He took him to a dense forest. At a certain place, he stopped and said the disciple to dig the ground. After digging a few feet down, he found a casket. The saint said, "Inside this there is Parasmani stone that can turn any ordinary metal into precious gold if touched and that is yours now." The disciple being so learnt, thought that if there would have been any relevancy of what the saint said, the iron casket would have been changed into gold. Musing this he threw the casket, but as he returned back where he found the casket, it had been turned into gold. It was coated with cloth inside it that restricted the contact of the casket to the stone. Regretting his deed he started searching for the stone that had lost in dry leaves when he threw the casket. He wore a gloomy face.

Moral : Crying over spilt milk is futile.

88. The Internet does not Matter Much

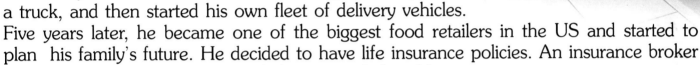

Once an HR manager of a company interviewed a jobless boy who had applied for the position of office boy and asked him to clean the floor as a test. The manager hired him and asked his e-mail address. Just as he said that he didn't have any computer or E-mail address, the manager threw the boy out of the office saying that no e:mail meant no existence and without existence he couldn't have a job. Then the boy went to the supermarket with $10 in pocket and bought 10 kg tomatoes. Then he sold them. Within two hours, he succeeded to double his capital. He repeated the operation and within two years, his money increased from which he bought a cart, then a truck, and then started his own fleet of delivery vehicles. Five years later, he became one of the biggest food retailers in the US and started to plan his family's future. He decided to have life insurance policies. An insurance broker shocked to know, without e-mail, he succeeded in life.

Moral : Scarcities embellish you.

89. Invitation

Once, a lady invited three long-bearded men named Wealth, Love and Success, who were sitting in front of her house. Although she didn't recognize them yet she said to come inside for a meal. Since her husband was not at home, so they denied to go inside. When her husband came, the woman invited them again. But they replied that

they never visit anywhere together and asked whom she wanted to invite. The lady said 'Wealth', but her husband wanted 'Success'. Their daughter-in-law was listening from the corner of the house and she came with her own suggestion and asked 'Love' to be invited in. The woman went out and asked 'Love' to come in, but got amazed to see that 'Wealth' and 'Success' also went inside the home with 'Love'. Then she said, "I only invited 'Love', not all." They replied, "Since you invited 'Love', so we will also go with him. Wherever there is 'Love', there are also 'Wealth' and 'Success'."

Moral : Love brings wealth and success.

90. The King's Repartee

King Nassreddin was conspicuously famous for his wit and eloquence. Once three wise man came to examine the intelligence of the king. The first wise man asked, "Where is the exact centre of the world?" The king replied, "Under my right foot." "How can you prove?" asked the man. Then the king replied, "If you don't believe, measure and see." The man became silent; now it was the turn of the 2nd man. He asked, "How many stars are there in the sky?" The king replied, "As many as there are hairs on my donkey." The wise man asked, "How you can say that?" "If you don't believe me, go and count the hairs of my donkey." The wise man could not say anything. Now the third man came forward to ask, "How many hairs are there in your donkey's tail?" "There are as many hairs in its tail as there are in your beard," the king replied. The man again said, "How do you know that?" "You can pull one hair out of my donkey's tail for each I pull out of your beard. If the hairs on my donkey's tail do not come to an end exactly at the same time as the hairs in your beard, I will admit that I was wrong," the king replied.

Moral : Silly questions should be solved with cleverness.

91. Knowledge of Truth

Once, a man sent his five sons in search of truth. After many years they returned. That time the man was going to die. He asked his sons, "Did you know what truth is?" His first son said, 'Yes' and started to recite the prayers of God. His second son started to give the example of the Upanishads. The third son started to give the lesson of the Vedas. His fourth son also said about many gods. But when the turn of the fifth son came, he didn't say anything. Father got up from his bed and again asked, but still he didn't say anything. Father again asked, "Did you know about truth or not?" But the son again remained silent. Then father closed his eyes and said, "One who knows, doesn't say anything, and one who doesn't know anything, says everything. I am happy that one of my sons has known about truth." Saying this father became silent and said, "Now I can die peacefully."

Moral : True knowledge is real, not fake.

92. The Lady with Sapphire

A wise woman was travelling in a country. On the way, she found a precious sapphire in a stream. Next day, she met another traveller who was very hungry. The wise woman opened her bag to share her food. The hungry traveller saw the precious stone inside the tattered bag and asked the woman to give it to him. She did so without hesitation. The traveller left, rejoicing his good fortune. He knew the stone was worth enough to give him security for a lifetime. But a few days later he came back to return the stone to the wise woman. The traveller said, "I've been thinking how valuable the stone is, but I give it back in the hope that you can give me something even more precious. Give me what you have within you that enabled you to give me the stone."

Moral : Satisfaction is more precious than sapphire.

93. Life and Money

A well-known speaker with $20, started a seminar in the room of 200 students and asked who would like that $20. All raised their hands, but crumbling the note he asked who still wanted it. Still, the hands were up in the air. Again, he dropped the $20 on the ground and started to grind it into the floor with his shoe. Picking a filthy and crumbled note he asked again, "Who still wants it?" Still, the hands went up into the air. Then he started to describe the main purpose doing that, "My friends, we have all learnt a very valuable lesson. No matter what was done to the money, it was still wanted because it did not decrease in value. It was still worth $20. Many times in our lives, we are dropped, crumpled and ground into the dirt by the decisions we make for the circumstances that come in our way. We may feel as though we are worthless. But we would not feel disheartened even in face of dangers."

Moral : Our life is as significant as money.

94. The Lion and the Deer

One day a deer went to a pool to quench his thirst. The pool water was so clear that he could see his reflection in it. He looked at the image of his antlers and felt proud of their beauty. Suddenly, his eyes fell on the reflection of his fore-legs. Though slender to look at, they gave him his high speed. But he felt sad seeing them. With a heavy heart, he quenched his thirst. Hardly had he raised his head when he saw a lion coming towards him. So, he took to his heels and the lion was left far behind. The deer took a sigh of relief. But unfortunately, his antlers got caught in a thicket. He tried his best to be free but could not. In the meantime, the lion came quite closer. The deer now cursed himself for condemning his legs and praising his horns. But now he could do nothing. The lion overtook him and tore him to pieces.

Moral : Appearances are often deceptive.

95. The Miserly Merchant

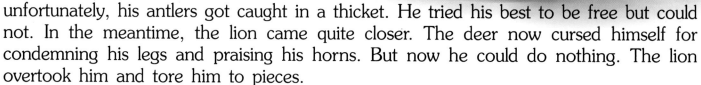

Once there was a merchant having a lot of gold. He melted it down in a lump and buried it in a pit. He was very happy that he had hidden his gold safely. So, he kept gloating over his treasure almost all the time. He used to visit the spot regularly where he had hidden the gold. One of his friends was keeping an eye on him and one day he discovered the secret. And one night, he went to the pit and dug the gold lump for himself. On his next visit to the spot, the merchant lamented on finding no gold over there. Hearing his cries, one of his neighbours came to him and asked what the matter was. The merchant replied, "I am ruined. Someone has stolen my treasure." The neighbour consoled him and said, "Your money was lying useless. Now, at least it will be of use to someone else."

Moral : Unused riches are useless.

96. The Mysterious Seed

Once a king's deteriorating health led him to take a decisive step of choosing a responsible king for kingdom. So he summoned all the adults of his kingdom and gave each a seed. The adults were said to come after one year with healthy plants, so the best blossomed plant would decide the next king of the kingdom. All the adults happily left the court with a hope of becoming the king. A boy among them, Roshan, sowed the seed, watered regularly and took great care of the plant but he felt daunted to see no growth in the seed. After one year, all the adults gathered with the flowery pots in their hands except Roshan, who brought mere an empty pot in his hands and felt embarrassed. The king observed the plants of all he had and stopped at once near Roshan and asked why an empty pot he was carrying. He shakingly answered that his one-year labour bore nothing. But he had been chosen as the king, as he had showed honesty. Actually, the king had given all the adults boiled seeds that couldn't be flourished into any plant.

Moral : Honesty makes you sublime.

97. Ramu, the Dreamer

Once, there was a beggar named Ramu, who used to go door to door to beg. From begging he had collected a pot full of flour, which he had kept hanging over his cot. One day after begging, he lay on his cot and started dreaming, gazing at that pot. He was dreaming that he would sell the flour and would get money. From that money he would buy a goat; that goat would bear many lamps. Then he would sell them and from that money he would buy a cow and the cow would bear calves. Then he would sell them and from that money he would buy precious jewels. And after becoming rich he would ask the king's daughter to marry him. After marrying the princess he would be more rich. Then from her wife he would have a son, who would be loved most but whenever he would do any mischievous work he would be punished. Suddenly, Ramu in his dream kicked his leg and his pot of flour fell down and broke into a thousand pieces. The flour scattered on the floor and got wasted.

Moral : Don't make castles in the air.

98. Retirement of the Mason

Once, an elderly mason was ready to retire. He told his contractor about his plans before leaving the house of the contractor to live a more leisurely life with his wife and enjoy his extended family. The contractor was sorry to see his diligent worker go and asked if he could build just one more house. The carpenter agreed, as it was his last task. But his heart was not in his work. He resorted to shoddy workmanship and used inferior materials. It was an unfortunate way to end a dedicated career. When the carpenter finished his work, his employer came to inspect the house. Then he handed the front-door key to the carpenter and said, "This is your house...my gift to you." The carpenter was shocked. If he had only known he was building his own house, he would have done it all so differently.

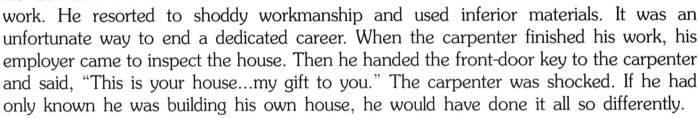

Moral : Never take your work lightly.

99. The Shrewd Wolves and the Foolish Dogs

Once upon a time, some dogs were guarding a flock of sheep. A wolf came there. The dogs became alert and started barking at him. The wolf could not dare to move ahead. But he was very shrewd. He went to the dogs and said, "We belong to the same family. So, we are very much alike. We only differ on one ground–that we wolves are free while you are slaves to your master. Let's forget our enmity and become friends." The dogs looked at one another and nodded. Seeing his clever idea work well, the wolf further said, "Accompany me to the forest; all the wolves will give you a warm welcome." Leaving the flock unguarded, the dogs went along with the wolf who took them to a den of wolves. The dogs entered the den and in no time the wolves fell upon them and tore them to pieces. Then the wolves went to the place where the flock was grazing. They killed all the sheep and ate them up.

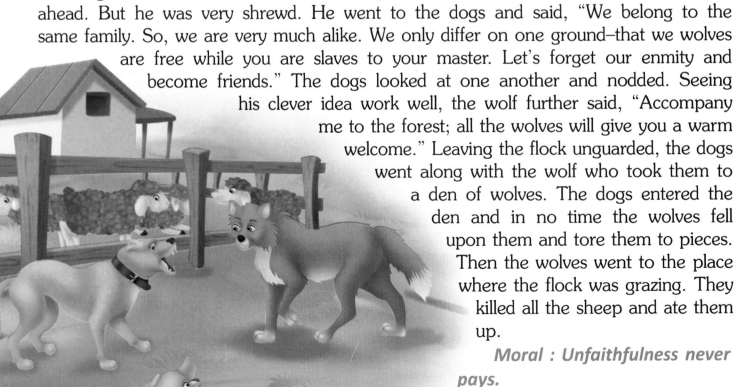

Moral : Unfaithfulness never pays.

100. *The Strange Sacrifice*

Once a king was ordered to construct a splendid temple within a week. So all sculptors assiduously worked hard but they got frustrated because in spite of working hard they were unable to complete the temple. Therefore, the king announced that if the temple would not be completed in an appropriate time then all sculptors would be killed. The sculptors got frightened because they didn't have time. One day, a twelve-year son of a sculptor, who was learning sculpture, also arrived at the working place of his father. There, he asked the permission of building the temple. First of all, they mocked on him but later agreed. Finally, the temple completed on the last day. But they were happy and sad also because they were frightened of the king because if it was known that a little boy had completed the temple in place of the sculptors, he would kill all the sculptors. Knowing this, the little boy decided to leave the village forever in order to save them.

Moral : Sacrifice makes you great.

101. *The Sweet Lover-boy and Father*

Once there was a boy who loved sweets very much. He demanded all the time with his poor father, who could not always afford sweets for his son. Therefore, father decided to take his son to a saint who lived near by and asked him to dissuade his son from asking sweets. The father with his son went to the saint and said, "O great saint, could you ask my son to stop asking for sweets which I cannot afford?" The great man was in difficulty; he told the man to bring his son back after one month. The boy and his father returned to the saint after a month. The saint asked the boy to stop asking sweets since his father couldn't afford them. From then onwards, the boy stopped asking for sweets. The boy's father asked the saint, "Why did you not ask my son to stop asking for sweets a month ago?" The saint replied, "How could I ask a boy to give up sweets when I also loved sweets myself?"

Moral : Words and actions should be the same.

102. The Balloon

Once there lived a little boy named Karan. He was very fond of playing with gas-filled balloons. One day he was playing with his friends. They had a bet. Each of them claimed that his balloon would go the highest in the sky. At a given signal, each of them let go of his balloon. All the balloons started going up in the sky. But Karan was disappointed to see that his balloon did not go the highest. On the third day, the children were playing the same game. But Karan was confused. He didn't know what colour of balloon to purchase. He approached the balloon-seller. Unable to decide, Karan asked the balloon-seller, "Tell me please, which balloon will go the highest in the sky?" The balloon-seller smiled at Karan and said, "My dear child! It is not the colour of the balloon that decides how high it will go in the sky. What matters the most is what the balloon has inside it." The balloon-seller then gave Karan the balloon that had more gas than the other balloons. That day Karan won the game and came home with a smile on his face.

Moral : How high a person will rise in life depends not on his caste, colour or creed, but on his thoughts, confidence, values and character.

103. The Clever Rabbit and the Elephant

A herd of elephants lived happily in a forest. One year, drought hit that area which caused many deaths. After a long search, they along with their leader Iravat got a lake at the far end of the forest. They decided to go there every day but they were unknown of the pity of the colony of rabbits. So every day, some rabbits got injured. The leader of rabbits sent Mikkoo, the cleverest rabbit, to convey a message to the elephants. So, Mikkoo introduced himself and said, "The lake belong to the Moon. He is very upset as you have crushed many rabbits on the way." Iravat agreed to that. When both reached the lake, the Moon was reflected in its still water. Just as Iravat dipped his trunk in the lake to greet the Moon, the water stirred and so did the Moon's reflection. "Oh! See how the mighty Moon shakes in anger," said Mikkoo. At this Iravat said in a mournful voice to forgive them and assured them that they would never come again to the lake nor ever harm the rabbits.

Moral : A lie that saves many lives is worth a thousand truths.

104. The Club 99

Long ago, a king looked unhappy in spite of having prosperity and luxury in his life. Pang of nostalgia always pervaded him. One day, the king felt amazed to see the cheerful servant, who always appeared with a contented face. The king summoned the servant, who revealed the secret of his happiness, *i.e.* his family's satisfaction with what he had. But he again called the minister to know broadly how an ordinary servant was living his life happily. "Majesty! It is the miracle of club 99. If you want to be happy, join it. Take a bag of 99 gold coins and leave them in front of the servant's house at night," the minister replied. The king did the same as the

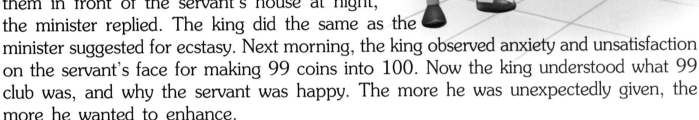

minister suggested for ecstasy. Next morning, the king observed anxiety and unsatisfaction on the servant's face for making 99 coins into 100. Now the king understood what 99 club was, and why the servant was happy. The more he was unexpectedly given, the more he wanted to enhance.

Moral : Desires never end and avarice brings uncertainty in life.

105. The Jackal's Treat

Once, a hunter, who was very well versed in archery, had gone to a forest to hunt a animal. Then he saw a boar and shot a sharp arrow directly to the boar's back. The arrow tore at the boar's back and caused a deep wound. In writhing pain and anger the wild boar rushed at the hunter and pierced his stomach with its sharp and pointed fangs. At once the proud hunter and the wild boar lay dead due to their injuries. After sometime a jackal passed from there and became happy to see such a wonderful feast.

The jackal proceeded to taste his succulent treat. Just as he bit into the boar's flesh, the pointed arrow pierced the top of his mouth and came out between his eyes. Soon the jackal too lay dead as the hunter and the boar.

Moral : Think twice before you act.

106. The Dalmatian and the Dolphin

A very proud sailor and his wife made a plan to go for a long journey through their splendid ship. Being her favourite and loving pet, she took her Dalmatian along with them. When they were far out at sea, a terrible storm overturned their ship.

Both the husband and the wife were caught in this tormented calamity and sank but luckily the dog, Dalmatian was saved and taken to the sea shore by a dolphin. Soon the dog reached the island on the dolphin's back who asked, "Do you know this place?"

The Dalmatian replied affirmatively, "One of my best friends is the king of this island. Do you know that I am actually a prince?" Knowing that no one lived on the island, the dolphin said, "Now you can be a king rather than a prince." The dog curiously asked how it was possible. The dolphin started swimming away. "As you are the only creature on this island, you will naturally be the king!" the dolphin answered.

Moral : Those who lie, dig holes for themselves.

107. Trust in God

Once, a man in cloudy weather with zero visibility was climbing. He was only a few feet away from the top of the mountain. He slipped and fell into the air, falling at a great speed. He kept falling and remembered all good and bad episodes of his life. While falling he was thinking how close death was getting. Suddenly he felt a rope tied to his waist. It pulled him very hard. Held only with a rope he requested God to help him. Just then a deep voice came from the sky, "What do you want me to do?" "Save me, God." "Do you really think I can save you?" "Of course I believe You can." "Then hold the rope tied to your waist tightly." There was a moment of silence and the man decided to hold onto the rope with all his strength. Next day, he was found alive, hanging and holding tight, from a rope. He was only one foot away from the ground.

Moral : Always keep faith in God.

108. The Conceited Disciple

An archer at a young age became proficient in archery. That made him so much conceited. He showed no gratitude towards his guru. One day, his guru asked him to accompany him to a mountainous place in quest of truth. In the midst of their journey they found a deep gulf which was difficult to pass through. There was a single, thin log which spanned the gulf. The guru reaching the middle of the log took his arrow out and shot it into a tree. Then his other shot cleaved the first arrow. Afterwards, he said to his young archer to do the same thing. But the boy could not do so as instructed by his guru. As a result, he could manage to stand on the thin log. He started trembling and asked for his guru's help. The guru saved his life and made him realize the importance of humility..

Moral : Don't be conceited after having power.

109. Two Strangers and the Old Man

Once a stranger entered a village and saw an old man. Then he asked the old man, "How are the people of his village? Are they good or cruel?" The old man didn't reply but asked him the same question, about the behaviour of the people of his village. Then the stranger replied angrily, "They are so cruel and bad." The old man replied that the villagers of his village were the same as the villagers of the stranger's village. After sometime another stranger came in the village and he also asked, "How are the people of the old man's village?" The old man again didn't reply but asked him the same question. Then the stranger replied that they were so generous and kind. The old man also said that the villagers of his village were also so kind and generous. Then the first stranger asked, "Why did you give the different answers to the same question." The old man replied, "You will be treated as you behave with others."

Moral : The world is like a mirror.

110. Who will Bell the Cat?

In the 20th century, in a palace, a king was really worried about the increasing number of rats, so he reared a cat, who could diminished the rats. The petrified rats called a meeting and decided to tie a bell in the cat's neck. But the cowardly rats couldn't do that and said that it was not involved mythological in their holy book to tie the bell, so they left the task. Fleeting time passed and there came the 21st century and a new generation of rats came who were clever-cum-intelligent. Their grandparents suggested to be alert of the cats, but the new generation promised to tie the bell. All were amazed and asked how they made it. They bravely replied that they went to a chemist shop, brought some sleeping pills and mixed them in the milk of the cat. When the cat drank and slept, they tied the bell.

Moral : Intelligence opens the path.

111. The Wolf and Sugarcane

Once upon a time, a wolf while wandering in a forest reached a field of sugarcane belonging to a farmer. But the fact is that wolves don't eat sugarcane. The wolf was about to move away when he saw a horse coming towards him. He decided to wait for him and extend a hand of friendship towards him. When the horse came, the wolf said to him, "Hello! Mr. Horse! How are you? See this fine field of sugarcane; I have left it untouched for you. I shall enjoy seeing you munching the ripe grains." The horse smiled and said, "Mr. Wolf! Had you been able to eat the sugarcane, you would not have thought of troubling your eyes at all. Rather you would have engaged in filling your appetite." The wolf felt highly ashamed and went away.

Moral : Don't gave others your useless appreciation.

112. The Woman and the Cock

A very pugnacious woman once lived in a village. All she had was only a cock that used to crow in the morning to wake people up. Her callousness really exasperated the inhabitants there. One day, the lady decided to leave the village but at the last time she cursed the village that there wouldn't be morning from next day, as the cock was being carried away who was the only source to awake the sun. She, in other village, thought the sun was glowing because of her cock. But after some days, she became sad to think that in her earlier village all would be living a life of darkness because the day appeared when her cock crowed but she had unknown of the fact that her cock crowed after the sun had risen.

Moral : Don't be pompous.

113. The Beggar and the King

Once a king was in his court when a young beggar came to him and asked for some money. He also said, "I am very poor; God hasn't given me anything. Please have mercy on me." Hearing this the king said, "Well, I will give you two gold coins but you will have to give me your both legs." Then the beggar replied, "If I would give you my legs then how I will walk." Then the king said, "If you can't give your legs then give me your both hands. For this, I will give you five gold coins." The beggar again denied giving his both hands. Now the king smiled and asked for his both eyes in exchange of 20 gold coins. Now the beggar got angry and said in exchange of even a thousand gold coins he would never give him his precious body parts. Then the king started laughing loudly and said, "If God has given such precious body parts then how can be you poor? You can do any work with them and earn money."

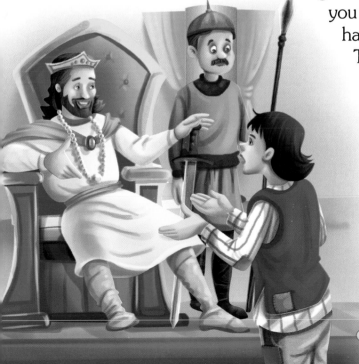

Moral : God has given us body as a precious gift.

114. A Father and his Four Sons

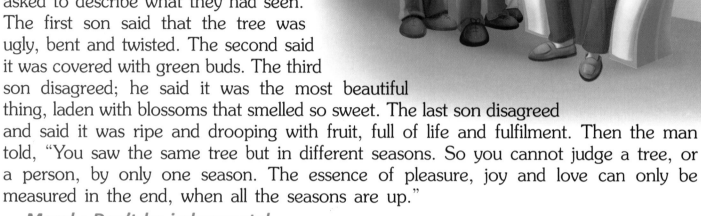

There was a man who had four sons. He wanted his son to teach not to judge things too quickly, so he sent them to look for a pear tree. The first son went in winter, the second in spring, the third in summer, and the youngest son in autumn. When they returned, he asked to describe what they had seen. The first son said that the tree was ugly, bent and twisted. The second said it was covered with green buds. The third son disagreed; he said it was the most beautiful thing, laden with blossoms that smelled so sweet. The last son disagreed and said it was ripe and drooping with fruit, full of life and fulfilment. Then the man told, "You saw the same tree but in different seasons. So you cannot judge a tree, or a person, by only one season. The essence of pleasure, joy and love can only be measured in the end, when all the seasons are up."

Moral : Don't be judgemental.

115. The Clever Fox

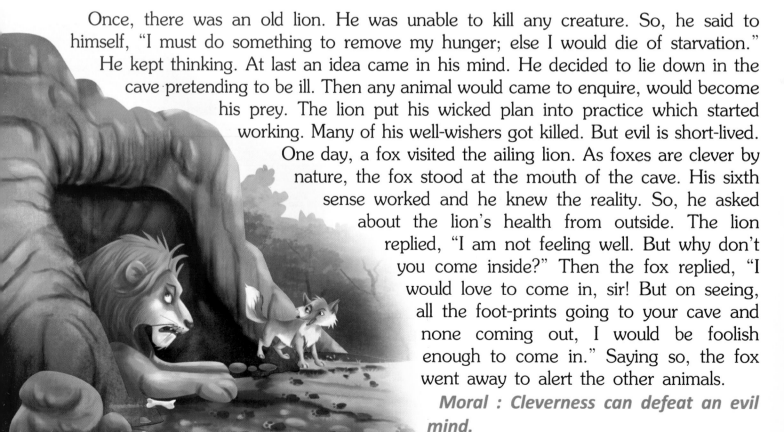

Once, there was an old lion. He was unable to kill any creature. So, he said to himself, "I must do something to remove my hunger; else I would die of starvation." He kept thinking. At last an idea came in his mind. He decided to lie down in the cave pretending to be ill. Then any animal would came to enquire, would become his prey. The lion put his wicked plan into practice which started working. Many of his well-wishers got killed. But evil is short-lived. One day, a fox visited the ailing lion. As foxes are clever by nature, the fox stood at the mouth of the cave. His sixth sense worked and he knew the reality. So, he asked about the lion's health from outside. The lion replied, "I am not feeling well. But why don't you come inside?" Then the fox replied, "I would love to come in, sir! But on seeing, all the foot-prints going to your cave and none coming out, I would be foolish enough to come in." Saying so, the fox went away to alert the other animals.

Moral : Cleverness can defeat an evil mind.

116. The Proud Lamp

Once a farmer bought a new lamp from the nearby market. When he reached home, it was dark. So, he filled the lamp with oil and putting a wick into it lighted it. It began to shine with a clear steady light. The lamp felt proud of itself and on its clear light. It started boasting that its light was brighter than that of the sun even. Suddenly a strong puff of wind came and blew it out. The lamp felt very small and realized its folly. It never knew that it could not face the wind at all. The farmer lighted the lamp once again. Now the lamp kept shining calmly showing no pride and making no boasts. The farmer said to the lamp, "Keep shining gently. Don't compare yourself to the sun. He never goes out, nor requires to be re-lighted like you."

Moral : Don't be disheartened to see others' progress.

117. The Jackal in The Lion's Family

Once, a lion and a lioness lived in the forest with their twin cubs. One day, the lion went to hunt for food but he didn't get anything. After wandering too long he found a jackal cub and brought him home. The lion said, "Today our cubs will eat the jackal cub as meal." Then the lioness disagreed to be so cruel and decided to bring it up as their son. So it came to be that the baby jackal stayed with the lion's family and grew into a young and healthy jackal. One day when out for their hunt the three encountered a mad elephant. The lion cubs, fearless as they were, approached the wild beast to kill it but the jackal said to them, "No brothers, do not go near him, for elephants are our enemy. You will be killed." Hearing this the valiant lion cubs lost courage and shrank back. At home they narrated the incident to the lioness who said, "You are still a jackal. Go away and join other jackals before it's too late."

Moral : A jackal remains a jackal.

118. The Eagle in the Hen's Nest

Once, an eagle had laid some eggs on a tree. Under the same tree a hen had laid eggs during the same period. One day, while the eagle had gone hunting, a bear climbed up the tree to eat the eagle's eggs. Hardly had the bear finished three of the eggs when the fourth one slipped off its hands and fell into the hen's nest. The hen which lived under the tree saw the eagle's egg by the side of her eggs. She felt pity on the eagle's egg, and decided to hatch it too. Soon the chicks began to grow. The chicks and the eaglet played together. Within no time the hen's chicks with the eagle's chick grew up. The eagle's chick never realized that it was an eagle and not a hen. Considering it a hen, the eagle ate the hen's food, walked and ran like other hens and made sounds like hens. The eagle never learnt to fly like other eagles and lived its whole life like a hen only.

Moral : Company makes you the same as they are.

119. The Extravagant Wife (story aur choti)

Once, a poor farmer had a young and beautiful wife. The wife was very extravagant. So they fought usually. One day the poor man's wife eloped with another man who pretended to be rich. The man was acutally a rogul who ran away with her jewellery. Just then a jackal came to the river bank with a large chunk of meat in his mouth. A hawk promptly swooped on the meat and flew away. The hawk's movement alerted the fish in the water and it too fled to the river bed. Thus, the jackal was left with nothing to eat. Seeing this the young wife laughed and said, "You fool, now you have neither the fish nor the meat to fill your hungry stomach." At this the Jackal sneered at the young woman and said, "You have lost your husband, your lover and your money. No one is so pitiable as you."

Moral : Desire for more may let you lose what you possess.

120. Work is Worship

There lived a man named Kranti who was well versed in making arrows. Whenever anybody saw his arrows, he never became tired to appreciate him. Once he was busy in making arrows. A procession of a rich person passed from there with lots of noise. He was so busy that his mind didn't distract from his work and he kept making the arrows. After sometime a saint passed from there. Till then Kranti had completed his work. The saint asked him, "Had you seen the procession of a rich man. How much time has passed after that procession?" Then Kranti said sorry to the saint and said he was too busy in making arrows so he couldn't see the procession. The saint replied that even if you were present, you didn't hear the sound of clarinets and drums. Then the man replied, "My work is worship for me. Whenever I do my work, I forget all things." These sentences made the saint to touch the feet of Kranti. The saint observed and said, "I will also try to do my work with full dedication."

Moral : One's work should be one's only worship.

121. The Bird in a Golden Cage

Long ago, a merchant was gifted a fragile bird with a melodious voice. He always took care of her and provided rich grains in a silver dish. He had placed her by his bed in a golden cage and became accustomed to listening to her songs in leisure. Once he had to go somewhere for business purpose, where he had to cross a forest, a bird's beloved habitat. So he asked his bird to deliver any message so that he might send her husband. She said, "She is despondent here; the golden palace can't give me the merriment which the freedom in Nature can. Please get me rid of here." Next day, he went for his work and reached the forest and conveyed her message but suddenly he found her husband lying down dead. The surprised merchant returned home and described all the incidents. His bird was dead that filled him with grief, so he took her out and patted her head to show his last love. Lo and behold! She was alive and flew away by saying that her beloved gave her idea to be free. She was glad now.

Moral : Freedom is necessary than luxury.

122. The Best Person

A prince was presented three dolls by a sage but this brought no exaltation to him. Rather, he was infuriated at the dolls and said to the sage that he was not a girl to be presented the dolls. The sage pacified him by saying that the dolls were for the future king who would have to take decisive steps in his life with his witty sense. Now he gave the prince a string to pass it through the hole of the ear of one of the dolls. The prince did so and found that it came out through the other side of the ear. Another string was given that came out of the mouth through the ear. The third string did not appear from anywhere else. The prince was perplexed. Then the sage described that the first doll represented a person who never retained anything. The second doll depicted the temperament of a person who was never loyal to his master. The third doll described a person who was indifferent to any views and thoughts. The sage further explained that the best person in the world is the one who accepts everything, speaks out when it is necessary, and pays attention to petty things.

Moral : To be trustworthy, a man must know when not to listen to petty things , when to remain silent and when to speak out.

123. The Earth's Angel Mother

Once upon a time, there was a child ready to be born. One day, the child eagerly asked God, "Being so small and helpless how will I live on earth?" God replied, "Among the many angels I have chosen one for you. She will be waiting for you and will take care of you." The child again asked who would make him feel happy on earth; how he would be able to understand the language of others, who would protect him? Then God requesting the child not to worry because that angel would be always with him who would talk to him, protect him and make him feel happy. At that moment there was much peace in Heaven, but voices from earth could already be heard. The child in a hurry, asked softly, "O God, if I am about to leave now please tell me my angel's name!" God replied, "Your angel's name is of no importance; you will simply call her MOTHER."

Moral : Mother is that angel whose presence on earth is priceless.

124. The Travellers and the Tree

Once two travellers were on their way on a scorching summer day. Since it was a sweltering sunny day, they felt too exhausted to proceed any more. So they decided to take a rest. They saw a large tree near by. Reclining under the tree, a traveller contemptuously condemned the tree for not having any fruits and nuts which could be eaten. Even its wood was useless. Then in a curt voice the tree replied, "You shouldn't be ungrateful to me; it's my thick branches in which you both are shielded from the burning rays of the sun at this moment." They felt ashamed of their words and took an oath not to belittle any creation of God.

Moral : All the creations of the world have a good purpose. We should venerate and understand their values.

125. Thirty Gold Coins

A very selfish and greedy man Harmu went to his kind friend Ramu to tell his misery of losing thirty gold coins. After some days, Ramu's daughter told his father that she found a bag containing 30 gold coins. Ramu's benevolent nature made her return that bag to Harmu. But Harmu refused to take it by saying that his daughter had stolen 10 coins. There were 40 coins in the bag. A dire situation of quibble led

them to the court, where the judge called Ramu's daughter by considering upon the whole matter and asked her to reveal the truth. "I had found only 30 coins," the girl replied. The judge observed, "Since she has found a bag of 30 coins, so this bag does belong to Ramu's daughter." Then Harmu confessed that he lied and he lost thirty gold coins but the judge did not listen to him.

Moral : Dishonesty snatches everything you have.

126. *Two Friends in Desert*

Once two friends were walking through the desert. During the journey they had an argument, and one friend slapped on the other's cheek. The one who got slapped was hurt, but without saying anything, wrote in the sand, "Today my best friend slapped me." They arrived at an oasis while walking, where they decided to take a bath. The one, who had been slapped, got stuck in the mire and started drowning, but the friend saved him. After the friend had recovered from drowning, he wrote on a stone, "Today my best friend saved my life." The friend who had slapped and saved his best friend asked him, "After I had hurt you, you wrote in the sand and now you write on a stone; why?" The other friend replied, "When someone hurts us, we should write it down in sand where the winds of forgiveness can erase it. But when someone does good for us, we must engrave it in a stone where no wind can ever erase it."

Moral : Be grateful to someone who helps you.

127. *Victory over Defeat*

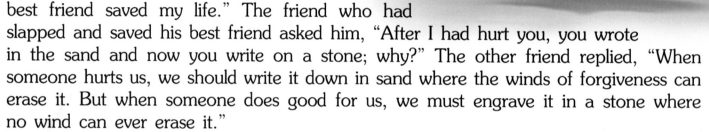

Sometime, even an assiduous work done follows mistakes that give fragile disappointment and discomfiture, but it doesn't mean the whole work is ruined or our labour went in vain with a futile attempt. One day, an ordinary scientist named Thomas Alva Edison used two thousand materials in search of a filament for the light bulb. The first time in his experiment he didn't succeed and some faults resisted him to achieve. Yet, he diligently tried again and again. But all his efforts didn't lead to complacency. Then his assistants scornfully said, "All our work has gone in vain and success wouldn't be in our favour." Edison retained his composure and told, "This mistake taught us a lesson that these two thousand materials can't be used for making a good light bulb." Now that scientist is remembered as a great inventor of the bulb. His indomitable will made him a predominant scientist.

Moral : Practice makes you perfect.

128. The Wise King

In a country, kings had to follow a ritual to leave their possessions and place after one year's reign. They had to face imminent fear of spending the rest of their life in a remote island, littered with dense forests and scary creatures. The same thing happened with a king after one year, who was attired in expensive clothes and lifted on an elephant for the farewell to the island. People were anxious for the next king. At the very time they saw a ship with a man that had sunk recently. They chose him as a new king. When the king was told about the rules, he decreased extravagancy of the kingdom and utilized all money in transforming the island into an abode so that he might live there. Now the same island flourished as a garden and many domestics were sent there for rearing. Even he kept his earning safe for future provisions. Now the day came when he had to visit the island but his cheers unlike the other kings, amazed the people. Actually, the wise king, being very visionary, thought for his future, which presented him a happy life.

Moral : Wisdom can deceive fate.

129. Wolf came! Wolf came!

Once upon a time, a shepherd boy looked after a flock of sheep. One day, he got into rut while driving the sheep and decided to play a trick on the dwellers of the village. He shouted, "Wolf came! Wolf came." The villagers heard his cries and threw themselves towards him to help the shepherd boy. When they approached him, the villagers went ballistic not to find any wolf over there. He laughed mockingly at them, "Ha, Ha, Ha! I be fooled all of you; I was only playing a trick on you." The villagers funningly returned back. A few days later, the boy played the same trick and cried, "Wolf! Wolf." Again as usual, they found nothing and in rage returned back. The shepherd befooled villagers many a time. The villagers found him mischievous. Once a wolf really arrived in the field and attacked one of the sheep of the shepherd. The boy cried for help but no villagers went to help him. When they came, it was too late to save many of his sheep.

Moral : We should never tell a lie to be fool others.

130. The King and the Boy

Once a king named Kushwant Singh, who was brave as well as kind too, was going somewhere with his soldier. Suddenly a piece of stone struck his head and he started bleeding. Seeing this the king got baffled and ordered his soldier to find the culprit. The soldier saw a twelve-year old boy and brought him in front of the king. The king asked, "Why did you do so?" Then the boy started crying and confessed his fault and said that he had been ravenous for three days; he was trying to pluck the mangoes from the tree by throwing the stone. When the king heard this he ordered his soldier to give the boy two gold coins. The boy happily took the coins and went from there. After that, the soldier asked, "In spite of being a culprit why was the boy given coins?" The king replied, "If a tree can give fruit after being hurt, why can't I give him coins after being struck with a stone."

Moral : Be generous and kind-hearted.

131. The Man and the Rose

Once a man planted and watered a rose plant faithfully before it blossomed. He examined it and saw the buds that would soon blossom, but the presence of sharp thorns around the buds made him furiously angry and he cut the thorns. But after some days again, he noticed those thorns. After that day he didn't take care of the plant. Still, the rose blossomed which made him baffled. Hastily, he went to a saint to ask the secret behind that. The saint made him understand by giving the best example of soul. He said, "The rose is like the soul of each person. Around the soul there are some shortcomings but it doesn't mean that we should leave our soul. This is one of the characteristics of love...to look at a person, know his true faults and accept that person into your life. Help others to realize and teach to overcome their faults. If we show them the 'rose' within themselves, they will conquer their thorns. Only then will they blossom many times."

Moral : Accept your shortcomings as well.

132. The Starfish

Once a boy saw an old man in the distance while walking down in a deserted Mexican beach at sunset. As he drew nearer, he noticed that his local native kept leaning down, picking something and throwing into the sea. As the boy came closer to him, he became puzzled to see that the local native was throwing the starfish back into the sea which had washed up on the beach. Then the boy asked the man reason for doing this. The man replied that they had been washed up on the beach. If he didn't throw them into the sea, they would die from lack of oxygen. The boy said again, "But there must be a thousand of starfish which have been washed up on the shore. You can't possibly get to all of them. You can't possibly make a difference." The local native smiled, bent down and picked up yet another starfish. As he threw it back into the sea, he replied, "I can make a difference to that one!"

Moral : Do good and forget.

133. The Crab and the Snake

Once there was a boy named Brahmdutt. One day, he had to go to a nearby village. As he was preparing to go there, his mother said to him, "You should not go alone; you must have someone with you." But Brahmdutt disagreed, and was about to move. Then his mother gave him a box saying that there was some food in it. Taking the box he proceeded. After walking a little bit he felt exhausted and decided to take a nap under a tree. Keeping that box he slept there, but there lived a snake in a hole. Brahmdutt's mother had secretly given him a box of camphor along with a crab. The snake came out of the hole smelling the camphor. When the snake opened the box, a crab came out and killed the snake. When Brahmdutt woke up and saw the snake and the crab, he understood that his mother had given the box of camphor and crab. He gave her thanks from his heart.

Moral : Don't ignore elders' advice.

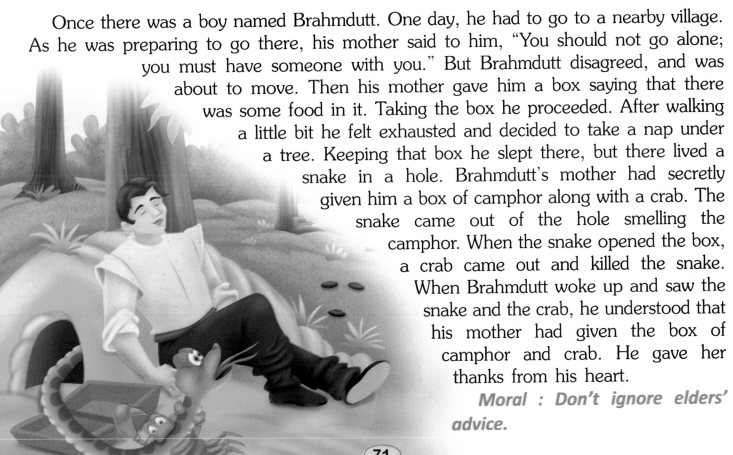

134. The Fisherman with his Flute

Once there was a fisherman who was a very good flutist as well. When he played on his flute, animals gathered around him to hear the sweet notes of his flute. One day, the fisherman thought to try his flute on the fish too. He was sure that the notes of his flute would attract the fish and they would come to him jumping out of the water. So, he went fishing taking his flute with him. He sat on a rock lying on the bank and began to play sweet tunes. He kept playing the flute for a long time but not even a single fish came out. The fisherman felt disappointed. He threw his flute on one side and cast his net into the water. Soon he was able to catch a great number of fish. He put them on the shore and they began to leap about for want of water. The angered fisherman said, "You rascals! You didn't come out when I played the flute so sweetly. Now you will dance when I play on my pipe. After all, you have no other choice."

Moral : For completing any tough work we should also be tough.

135. The Foolish Fisherman

Once, there was a big pond near a village. The villagers used the water of the pool for drinking and for other purposes as well. The pool abounded with fish. Once a fisherman went fishing to the pool. He spread his net into the pool and sat down. But he was very impatient. So, he tied a long string to a small stone. Then putting it into the pool, he began to stir the water to drive more fish into his net. A villager saw him do so and asked him not to make the water muddy. But the fisherman didn't listen to him and went on beating the water and making it dirty. Becoming so muddy and dirty, the fish started dying. Most of the fish died and now the only source of earning for the fisherman also mixed in mud. Now the fisherman was disgruntled to see this and started feeling guilty.

Moral : Don't be impatient.

136. *The Four Wives*

A king had four bewitchingly beautiful wives whom he loved very much. The fourth queen being so young was so attractive and gorgeous. The third wife had brought abundant wealth in her dowry. But the fourth queen was adorned much by the king. The second queen was so sagacious. She gave him a son, so he loved her a lot. But the first queen had lost her charm. Yet, she cared for the king selflessly. In spite of showing dedication the first queen was never given love by the king. Time passed; the king got a major injury in his belly and was in his last stage. Then the king asked all his queens to be his companions, but all the three pretended. The fourth one flew to her father's house. The third queen left his kingdom, the second one used her mind to escape, but the first queen pluckily agreed to go with him forever.

Moral : Actually, we all have four wives in our life. The fourth wife is our body, the third wife is our profession, the second wife is our family but the first wife is our soul that lives with us till death and never lets us feel alone.

137. *The Frog and the Mouse*

Once a frog lived in a marsh. Near by, there lived a mouse in a hole. They were good friends but one day they entered a dispute. Both of them claimed to be the owner of the marsh. The frog was stronger than the mouse but the mouse was very clever. He hid himself under the grass, attacked the frog and harmed him a lot. The frog, seeing this, decided to put an end to the dispute and challenged the mouse for a clash. Without any hesitation, the mouse accepted the challenge. Each of them had a point of reed to use it like a spear. Either of them was sure of his victory. When they were about to start fighting, a hawk came there flying. Hovering in the sky, she saw the animals ready for a duel. So, she swooped down, caught them both in her claws and carried them away to feed her young ones.

Moral : Disunity invites enemies.

138. Futile Labour

A callous dacoit was very notorious for robbing the people for his survival. Once he came to know that a saint had many valuable idols. He formulated a plan to plunder him. He took a sharp sword and went to the saint and said, "I have heard that you possess many costly idols; give them to me; otherwise, you would be beheaded." Listening to this he said, "If you need money, you should meet a king whom I know. He gives ten thousand gold coins as wage, but still there is one condition. You can neither dissipate the coins nor take them to the other country." The dacoit replied, "Do you think I am a foolish, who will work with such condition?" Then the saint replied, "So what do you think when you die? You would take these idols with you. Why do you perpetrate crime for something that is not yours?" Saying this he said that he could take the idols. But the dacoit was overwhelmed and realized his sin. After that, he left robbery forever.

Moral : Always tread onto the path of righteousness.

139. God's Blessing

Once, a most pious man who never gave pain to others lived happily in a village. All the people of that village conveyed their profound reverence for him and eulogized him as God. Everybody was in awe towards his attribute of being so generous.

To see this God himself came to him and gladly said, "Your selfless life compelled me to bless you, so you are being given a boon–a person will be free from all sufferings whom you touch." But the man denied to take it and said, "This is the work of deities." Then God presented other option and said, "You will be given magical power so that all sinners may transform into good humans in your contact." Again, the man rejected and said, "This is the work of prophets or angels, but I am a human and I am happy with my ordinary life." Hearing the words God felt astonished and gave him the blessing of being so noble forever and got vanished.

Moral : Everybody should respect others humans.

140. God's Real Devotee

A voyaging ship was wrecked during a storm at sea and only two of the men on it were able to swim to a small, desert like island. The two survivors found only prayer to be free from that place. To find out whose prayer was more powerful, they agreed to divide the territory between them and stay on the opposite sides of the island. A fruit bearing tree was shown when the first man prayed for food. The other man's parcel of land remained barren. After some days the first man felt lonely, so he prayed for a wife. Next day another ship was wrecked, and the only survivor was a woman who swam to his side of the land. On the other side of the island, there was nothing. Soon the first man prayed for a house, clothes, more food. Next day, like magic, all of these were given to him. The second man still had nothing. Finally, the first man asked for a ship and decided to leave the place thinking that the second person's prayer was not heard. Then he heard a voice, 'Why are you leaving your companion on the island?' His only wish was, 'All yours prayers should be answered.'

Moral : True prayers work wonder.

141. The Goldsmith and the Crow

Once, a great saint was on his way for alms. He visited each house of the village. He reached the door of a goldsmith, who was polishing gold balls. The saint was heartily invited and was given reverence. The saint sat and the goldsmith went inside to bring some fruits for the saint. Meanwhile, a crow came and swallowed 3 balls of gold. When the goldsmith came back, he got astonished to see the less number of gold balls and brutally humiliated the saint. He tied him by accusing him of theft in scorching sunlight that led to the saint's death but the saint didn't say anything about the crow.

In the evening when the sun was setting, lots of crows were crossing the goldsmith's house. Suddenly, the goldsmith found three gold balls which were dropped by a crow. He understood the whole situation that jolted him. Now the goldsmith repented of his folly. The saint had died for the sake of the crow's life.

Moral : A saint teaches us to live for others.

142. Hard Labour

Two very fast friends Som and Nero lived in a village. They both were farmers but one year a severe drought occurred in their part of the country. The rain had failed and only one way to irrigate their field was to join a stream through a canal by digging ground. Som, a very valiant person, determined to dug the ground till it was connected to the stream. Both friends Som and Nero started but Nero, being so capricious, went home when he was called for lunch. But when Som's wife came to call him for lunch, by rebuking he said, "I work the whole day so that you may be fed the whole year." And he kept his hard labour up for three days. When the work was done of joining the canal through the stream he returned home and had dinner. His lifeless grains were again dancing with joy. Meanwhile, Nero's idleness drew him again to the field where all his crops were already dead.

Moral : Hard labour is always fruitful.

143. The Lion's Blind Love

Once upon a time a farmer used to live in a cottage at the edge of a forest. He had a daughter who was very beautiful. A lion often used to see the pretty girl during his usual prowl and fell in love with her. So, one day, he went to the girl's father and asked for her hand. The man was unwilling to give his daughter to a fierce husband. But he didn't have the courage to refuse and offend the lion. So, he thought hard and hit upon a plan. He said to the lion, "My daughter is afraid of your teeth and sharp nails. She will marry you only if you let me have your teeth pulled out and your nails clipped." As the lion was blind in love with the girl, he at once agreed to the demand without thinking of the outcome. As a result, the lion was totally disarmed. The girl's father beat him with a heavy stick and drove him away.

Moral : Love is blind.

144. *The Most Beautiful Heart*

A large crowd gathered when a young man was proclaiming, having the most beautiful heart, without any flaw and mark; they all agreed. Suddenly, an old man appeared at the front of the crowd and said, "Your heart is not nearly so beautiful as mine." The young man laughed and said, "Compare your heart with mine. Mine is perfect and yours is a mess of scars and tears." Then the old man replied, "Every scar represents a person to whom I have given my love. I tear out a piece of my heart and give it to them...and often they give me a piece of their heart which fits into the empty place in my heart. But because the pieces aren't exact, I have some rough edges, which I cherish, because they remind me of the love we shared." Hearing this the young man agreed, and then took a piece from his old scarred heart and placed it in the wound in the young man's heart. It fit but not perfectly, as there were some jagged edges. The young man looked at his heart, not perfect any more but more beautiful than ever, since love from the old man's heart flowed into his.

Moral : Physical appearance can't be real appearance.

145. *The Woodcutter and the Shepherd*

A deeply deaf shepherd was driving 11 sheep in a forest. Daily his wife bought meal for him but one day she didn't come. So to know about her welfare the shepherd hastily took departure for his house. Then he saw a woodcutter climbing on a tree whom he said to take care of his sheep. Unfortunately, the woodcutter was also deaf; he didn't understand his message and gave a negative answer by hand movement. But the shepherd thought that he agreed to care. When the shepherd returned, he counted his sheep and pleasingly gave a sheep of broken leg to the woodcutter as a gift. The woodcutter thought that the shepherd was abusing him for breaking the sheep's leg, so they both started to quibble over that, without understanding each other. Meanwhile, a saint was passing by; he understood the whole matter and pacified the situation and said to them to do their own work.

Moral : We only hear, whatever we want to hear.

77

146. The Hungry Fox

Once upon a time, a ravenous fox was looking for something to eat. He worked too hard but couldn't find food. Finally, he went to the edge of the forest and searched there for food. Suddenly, he caught sight of a big tree with a hole in it. Seeing a package in the hole the fox jumped into the hole, thinking that there must be food in it. The fox became exhilarated to see a lot of food in that package. An old woodcutter had placed the food in the tree trunk while cutting trees in the forest. The fox happily demolished the food. After eating he felt thirsty, so he decided to leave the trunk and have some water from a nearby spring. The fox tried hard, but couldn't get out of the hole. Because of eating too much, he had become too big to come out of the hole. The fox became very sad and upset.

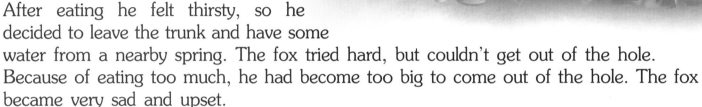

Moral : Before doing something we should think again and again.

147. The Tree that Lived for others

Once upon a time, there were two trees in a forest. One tree was very generous in sharing its fruits with birds and other creatures. The other tree, being of the opposite nature, was very selfish. Finally, in a couple of years the selfish tree lost all its leaves and became thin and weak. The other tree, unselfish as ever, kept growing and bore fruit aplenty. By now, the selfish tree had realized that the cause of its plight was its selfishness. It soon became unselfish and began inviting birds and other creatures with a smile. Before long, it grew in health and became bountiful like the other tree.

Moral : However capable or intelligent one may be, one grows only with others.

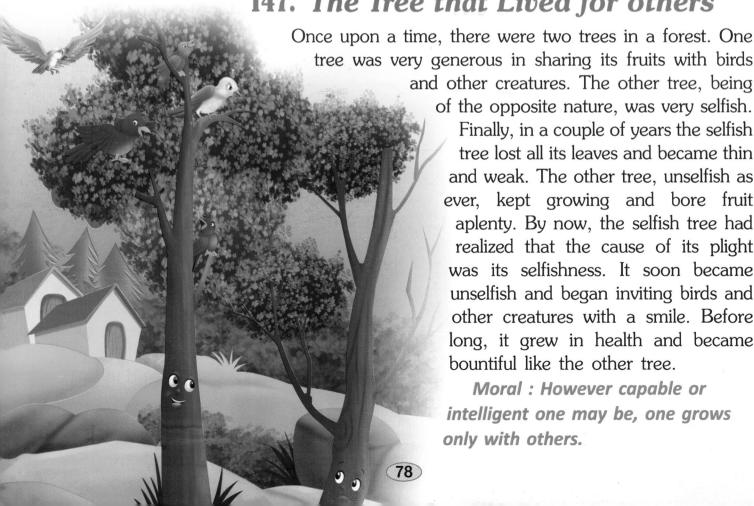

148. *End of the Evil Mind*

There was a cruel king who always believed in persecuting his subjects and expanding his status with the money which was for the welfare of his subjects. One day, to their utter amazement, the subjects found the king to be intensely benevolent and benign. The president asked the king about his transformation. Thereupon the king stated that once he was going through the forest. He noticed a fox was being chased by a hound. Ultimately, the hound bit in the fox's leg. Meanwhile, a passer-by threw a heavy stone at the hound. It broke the hound's leg. Now it was the turn of the passer-by who was kicked by a horse when he was returning to his house. The horse lost its balance and fell down into a pit. That day he realized that bad things are cursed with bad mishap for sure. Immersed in deep thought, the king did not see the steps in front of him and fell down, breaking his neck.

Moral- Bad things have a bad effect.

149. *The Superstitious Stag Family*

Once, a father stag, a mother stag and their baby stag had gone for an outing, in a jungle. All of a sudden, the antlers of the father stag got caught in the overhanging branches of a tree. The stag struggled hard, but could not free himself. Now the father stag started cursing his fate that how unlucky he was. Next morning, a woodcutter who came along saw the stag with his antlers entangled with the branches. Soon, the woodcutter set the stag free. On reaching home the stag was shocked to see that lions had attacked their area, the previous day. Many friends of the stag were killed. But he and his family were saved.

Moral : Don't be superstitious.

150. The Wife

Once there was a man who used to beat his wife mercilessly, but unfortunately she succumbed to his beating though he had not intended to kill her. When she died, he apprehensively came out of his house and met an acquaintance to whom he posed his problem. His friend advised him to invite a young man to his house, behead him and put the head next to the wife's corpse. Then the wife's relatives could be explained that he slew them acrimoniously as they were seen together on bed. The man did the same and beheaded a young man in his house and told a fictitious story to his wife's relatives. The advisor had a son who hadn't reached home that day. Not finding him he got baffled. Then he came to the house of the one whom he had offered evil advice and asked him if he carried out the plan suggested by him. He astonished to see his own son as the beheaded young man.

Moral : Evil thoughts distract the mind.

151. The Indomitable Will

Jhon Roebling, a valiant and creative engineer, was determined to build a spectacular bridge connecting New York with the long island. He was being aided by his son, Washington, who did never let him feel daunted. The construction being very difficult to do attracted a very few workers to perform the task. However, the project was resumed and went in the right direction for a few months. But soon, a tragic accident on the site took place that had snatched the life of Jhon Roebling and left Washington to die. After a few months, recovery he was again embued with a strong feeling to complete his dad's dream. That time all he could do was to move one finger and he decided to make the best of it. By moving this, he slowly developed a code of communication with his wife that furthur helped him give instructions to the engineers. A great hard work of 13 years brought the colours of happiness as BROOKLYNE BRIDGE, that stood as glory and triumph of father and son, made them worldwide famous.

Moral : Determination does a miracle.